Subaltern Movements in India

Social struggles in India target both the state and private corporations. Three subaltern struggles against development in Gujarat, India, succeeded, to varying degrees, due to legalism from below and translocal solidarity, but that success has been compromised by its gendered geographies.

Based on extensive field research, this book examines the reasons for the three social movements' success. It analyzes the contradictory reality of the deepening of democracy along with coercive state measures in the era of neoliberal development, the importance of the legal changes in the state, the nature of the local fields of protest, and the translocal field of protest in contemporary subaltern protests. Addressing gender inequalities within and outside the struggle, the author shows that despite subaltern women having symbolic visibility in the public spaces of the struggles – such as rallies, protests, and meetings with government officials – they are absent from the private spaces of decision making and collective dialogues.

This book offers a new approach to the politics of social movements in contemporary India by discussing the nuanced relationship between development and democracy, social justice, and gender justice. It will be of interest to academics in the field of development and gender studies, studies of social movements, and South Asian studies.

Manisha Desai is an associate professor of sociology and women's studies at the University of Connecticut. Her research interests include gender, globalization and development, transnational feminisms, and contemporary Indian society.

Routledge Contemporary South Asia Series

1 **Pakistan**
Social and cultural transformations in a Muslim nation
Mohammad A. Qadeer

2 **Labor**
Democratization and development in India and Pakistan
Christopher Candland

3 **China–India Relations**
Contemporary dynamics
Amardeep Athwal

4 **Madrasas in South Asia**
Teaching terror?
Jamal Malik

5 **Labor, Globalization and the State**
Workers, women and migrants confront neoliberalism
Edited by Debdas Banerjee and Michael Goldfield

6 **Indian Literature and Popular Cinema**
Recasting classics
Edited by Heidi R.M. Pauwels

7 **Islamist Militancy in Bangladesh**
A complex web
Ali Riaz

8 **Regionalism in South Asia**
Negotiating cooperation, institutional structures
Kishore C. Dash

9 **Federalism, Nationalism and Development**
India and the Punjab economy
Pritam Singh

10 **Human Development and Social Power**
Perspectives from South Asia
Ananya Mukherjee Reed

11 **The South Asian Diaspora**
Transnational networks and changing identities
Edited by Rajesh Rai and Peter Reeves

12 **Pakistan–Japan Relations**
Continuity and change in economic relations and security interests
Ahmad Rashid Malik

13 **Himalayan Frontiers of India**
Historical, geo-political and strategic perspectives
K. Warikoo

14 India's Open-Economy Policy
Globalism, rivalry, continuity
Jalal Alamgir

15 The Separatist Conflict in Sri Lanka
Terrorism, ethnicity, political economy
Asoka Bandarage

16 India's Energy Security
Edited by Ligia Noronha and Anant Sudarshan

17 Globalization and the Middle Classes in India
The social and cultural impact of neoliberal reforms
Ruchira Ganguly-Scrase and Timothy J. Scrase

18 Water Policy Processes in India
Discourses of power and resistance
Vandana Asthana

19 Minority Governments in India
The puzzle of elusive majorities
Csaba Nikolenyi

20 The Maoist Insurgency in Nepal
Revolution in the twenty-first century
Edited by Mahendra Lawoti and Anup K. Pahari

21 Global Capital and Peripheral Labour
The history and political economy of plantation workers in India
K. Ravi Raman

22 Maoism in India
Reincarnation of ultra-left wing extremism in the twenty-first century
Bidyut Chakrabarty and Rajat Kujur

23 Economic and Human Development in Contemporary India
Cronyism and fragility
Debdas Banerjee

24 Culture and the Environment in the Himalaya
Arjun Guneratne

25 The Rise of Ethnic Politics in Nepal
Democracy in the margins
Susan I. Hangen

26 The Multiplex in India
A cultural economy of urban leisure
Adrian Athique and Douglas Hill

27 Tsunami Recovery in Sri Lanka
Ethnic and regional dimensions
Dennis B. McGilvray and Michele R. Gamburd

28 **Development, Democracy and the State**
Critiquing the Kerala model of development
K. Ravi Raman

29 **Mohajir Militancy in Pakistan**
Violence and transformation in the Karachi conflict
Nichola Khan

30 **Nationbuilding, Gender and War Crimes in South Asia**
Bina D'Costa

31 **The State in India after Liberalization**
Interdisciplinary perspectives
Edited by Akhil Gupta and K. Sivaramakrishnan

32 **National Identities in Pakistan**
The 1971 war in contemporary Pakistani fiction
Cara Cilano

33 **Political Islam and Governance in Bangladesh**
Edited by Ali Riaz and C. Christine Fair

34 **Bengali Cinema**
'An other nation'
Sharmistha Gooptu

35 **NGOs in India**
The challenges of women's empowerment and accountability
Patrick Kilby

36 **The Labour Movement in the Global South**
Trade unions in Sri Lanka
S. Janaka Biyanwila

37 **Building Bangalore**
Architecture and urban transformation in India's Silicon Valley
John C. Stallmeyer

38 **Conflict and Peacebuilding in Sri Lanka**
Caught in the peace trap?
Edited by Jonathan Goodhand, Jonathan Spencer and Benedict Korf

39 **Microcredit and Women's Empowerment**
A case study of Bangladesh
Amunui Faraizi, Jim McAllister and Taskinur Rahman

40 **South Asia in the New World Order**
The role of regional cooperation
Shahid Javed Burki

41 **Explaining Pakistan's Foreign Policy**
Escaping India
Aparna Pande

42 **Development-induced Displacement, Rehabilitation and Resettlement in India**
Current issues and challenges
Edited by Sakarama Somayaji and Smrithi Talwar

43 The Politics of Belonging in India
Becoming Adivasi
Edited by Daniel J. Rycroft and Sangeeta Dasgupta

44 Re-Orientalism and South Asian Identity Politics
The oriental Other within
Edited by Lisa Lau and Ana Cristina Mendes

45 Islamic Revival in Nepal
Religion and a new nation
Megan Adamson Sijapati

46 Education and Inequality in India
A classroom view
Manabi Majumdar and Jos Mooij

47 The Culturalization of Caste in India
Identity and inequality in a multicultural age
Balmurli Natrajan

48 Corporate Social Responsibility in India
Bidyut Chakrabarty

49 Pakistan's Stability Paradox
Domestic, regional and international dimensions
Edited by Ashutosh Misra and Michael E. Clarke

50 Transforming Urban Water Supplies in India
The role of reform and partnerships in globalization
Govind Gopakumar

51 South Asian Security
Twenty-first century discourse
Sagarika Dutt and Alok Bansal

52 Non-discrimination and Equality in India
Contesting boundaries of social justice
Vidhu Verma

53 Being Middle-class in India
A way of life
Henrike Donner

54 Kashmir's Right to Secede
A critical examination of contemporary theories of secession
Matthew J. Webb

55 Bollywood Travels
Culture, diaspora and border crossings in popular Hindi cinema
Rajinder Dudrah

56 Nation, Territory, and Globalization in Pakistan
Traversing the margins
Chad Haines

57 The Politics of Ethnicity in Pakistan
The Baloch, Sindhi and Mohajir ethnic movements
Farhan Hanif Siddiqi

58 Nationalism and Ethnic Conflict
Identities and mobilization after 1990
Edited by Mahendra Lawoti and Susan Hangen

59 **Islam and Higher Education**
Concepts, challenges and opportunities
Marodsilton Muborakshoeva

60 **Religious Freedom in India**
Sovereignty and (anti) conversion
Goldie Osuri

61 **Everyday Ethnicity in Sri Lanka**
Up-country Tamil identity politics
Daniel Bass

62 **Ritual and Recovery in Post-Conflict Sri Lanka**
Eloquent bodies
Jane Derges

63 **Bollywood and Globalisation**
The global power of popular Hindi cinema
Edited by David J. Schaefer and Kavita Karan

64 **Regional Economic Integration in South Asia**
Trapped in conflict?
Amita Batra

65 **Architecture and Nationalism in Sri Lanka**
The trouser under the cloth
Anoma Pieris

66 **Civil Society and Democratization in India**
Institutions, ideologies and interests
Sarbeswar Sahoo

67 **Contemporary Pakistani Fiction in English**
Idea, nation, state
Cara N. Cilano

68 **Transitional Justice in South Asia**
A study of Afghanistan and Nepal
Tazreena Sajjad

69 **Displacement and Resettlement in India**
The human cost of development
Hari Mohan Mathur

70 **Water, Democracy and Neoliberalism in India**
The power to reform
Vicky Walters

71 **Capitalist Development in India's Informal Economy**
Elisabetta Basile Serpl

72 **Nation, Constitutionalism and Buddhism in Sri Lanka**
Roshan de Silva Wijeyeratne

73 **Counterinsurgency, Democracy, and the Politics of Identity in India**
From warfare to welfare?
Mona Bhan

74 **Enterprise Culture in Neoliberal India**
Studies in youth, class, work and media
Edited by Nandini Gooptu

75 **The Politics of Economic Restructuring in India**
Economic governance and state spatial rescaling
Loraine Kennedy

76 **The Other in South Asian Religion, Literature and Film**
Perspectives on Otherism and Otherness
Edited by Diana Dimitrova

77 **Being Bengali**
At home and in the world
Edited by Mridula Nath Chakraborty

78 **The Political Economy of Ethnic Conflict in Sri Lanka**
Nikolaos Biziouras

79 **Indian Arranged Marriages**
A social psychological perspective
Tulika Jaiswal

80 **Writing the City in British Asian Diasporas**
Edited by Seán McLoughlin, William Gould, Ananya Jahanara Kabir and Emma Tomalin

81 **Post-9/11 Espionage Fiction in the US and Pakistan**
Spies and 'terrorists'
Cara Cilano

82 **Left Radicalism in India**
Bidyut Chakrabarty

83 **"Nation-State" and Minority Rights in India**
Comparative perspectives on Muslim and Sikh identities
Tanweer Fazal

84 **Pakistan's Nuclear Policy**
A minimum credible deterrence
Zafar Khan

85 **Imagining Muslims in South Asia and the Diaspora**
Secularism, religion, representations
Claire Chambers and Caroline Herbert

86 **Indian Foreign Policy in Transition**
Relations with South Asia
Arijit Mazumdar

87 **Corporate Social Responsibility and Development in Pakistan**
Nadeem Malik

88 **Indian Capitalism in Development**
Barbara Harriss-White and Judith Heyer

89 **Bangladesh Cinema and National Identity**
In search of the modern?
Zakir Hossain Raju

90 **Suicide in Sri Lanka**
The anthropology of an epidemic
Tom Widger

91 **Epigraphy and Islamic Culture**
Inscriptions of the Early Muslim Rulers of Bengal (1205–1494)
Mohammad Yusuf Siddiq

92 **Reshaping City Governance**
London, Mumbai, Kolkata, Hyderabad
Nirmala Rao

93 **The Indian Partition in Literature and Films**
History, politics, and aesthetics
Rini Bhattacharya Mehta and Debali Mookerjea-Leonard

94 **Development, Poverty and Power in Pakistan**
The impact of state and donor interventions on farmers
Syed Mohammad Ali

95 **Ethnic Subnationalist Insurgencies in South Asia**
Identities, interests and challenges to state authority
Edited by Jugdep S. Chima

96 **International Migration and Development in South Asia**
Edited by Md Mizanur Rahman and Tan Tai Yong

97 **Twenty-First Century Bollywood**
Ajay Gehlawat

98 **Political Economy of Development in India**
Indigeneity in transition in the state of Kerala
Darley Kjosavik and Nadarajah Shanmugaratnam

99 **State and Nation-Building in Pakistan**
Beyond Islam and security
Edited by Roger D. Long, Gurharpal Singh, Yunas Samad, and Ian Talbot

100 **Subaltern Movements in India**
Gendered geographies of struggle against neoliberal development
Manisha Desai

101 **Islamic Banking in Pakistan**
Shariah-compliant finance and the quest to make Pakistan more Islamic
Feisal Khan

Subaltern Movements in India
Gendered geographies of struggle
against neoliberal development

Manisha Desai

LONDON AND NEW YORK

First published 2016
by Routledge
2 Park Square, Milton Park, Abingdon, Oxon OX14 4RN

and by Routledge
711 Third Avenue, New York, NY 10017

First issued in paperback 2018

Routledge is an imprint of the Taylor & Francis Group, an informa business

© 2016 Manisha Desai

The right of Manisha Desai to be identified as author of this work has been asserted by her in accordance with sections 77 and 78 of the Copyright, Designs and Patents Act 1988.

All rights reserved. No part of this book may be reprinted or reproduced or utilised in any form or by any electronic, mechanical, or other means, now known or hereafter invented, including photocopying and recording, or in any information storage or retrieval system, without permission in writing from the publishers.

Trademark notice: Product or corporate names may be trademarks or registered trademarks, and are used only for identification and explanation without intent to infringe.

Every effort has been made to contact copyright holders for their permission to reprint material in this book. The publishers would be grateful to hear from any copyright holder who is not here acknowledged and will undertake to rectify any errors or omissions in future editions of this book.

British Library Cataloguing in Publication Data
A catalogue record for this book is available from the British Library

Library of Congress Cataloging-in-Publication Data
Desai, Manisha.
  Subaltern movements in India : gendered geographies of struggle against neoliberal development / Manisha Desai.
    pages cm. — (Routledge contemporary South Asia series)
  Includes bibliographical references and index.
  1. Marginality, Social—India. 2. Women—India—Social conditions. 3. Women in development—India.
  4. Neoliberalism—India. I. Title.
  HN683.5.D3664 2015
  305.48'20954—dc23
  2015016539

ISBN 13: 978-1-138-59299-5 (pbk)
ISBN 13: 978-1-138-93829-8 (hbk)

Typeset in Times New Roman
by Apex CoVantage, LLC

Contents

List of figures		xv
Acknowledgements		xvii
Glossary and abbreviations		xxi
1	Legalism from below, translocal fields of protest, and gendered geographies	1
2	The making of translocal fields of protest	26
3	Resisting displacement, challenging exclusion in Nar-Par Adivasi Sangathan	48
4	From strategic visibility to marginality in the Mahuva movement	74
5	Ongoing engagement in gender justice in MASS	103
6	Towards a gender-just development and democracy	130
	Appendix: the Par-Tapi-Narmada Link Project	141
	Index	147

For Ishan and Ilan Azaadi Adhuri Che

Figures

1.1	Map of Gujarat with the locations of the three struggles	2
3.1	People's court at Khadki *ashram* school	49
3.2	Booklet produced by the Sangathan for educating *adivasis* about the dams	57
3.3	Slogans from the booklet	58
3.4	Slogans from the booklet	59
4.1	Women walking along the highway during the *padyatra*	74
4.2	Nirma factory in the background and the reservoir in the foreground	80
4.3	Women resting during the *padyatra*	82
4.4	Women cooking *rotlas*, flatbread, at a rest stop during the *padyatra*	83
4.5	Men leading the *yatra*	85
4.6	Photos on one of the tractors accompanying the *yatra*	87
5.1	The OPG power plant under construction in Bhadreshwar, October 2013	104
5.2	Fisher communities on Randh *bandar*	109
5.3	Fish drying at Junna *bandar*	111
A.1	Par-Tapi-Narmada Link Project	141

Acknowledgements

Like the *yatras* in this book, the *yatra* of writing this book was also a lengthy endeavor that involved the support of many along the way. First and foremost are the subaltern women and men who embarked on the struggles that animate this book. Without their activism, there would be no book. Their work, as I show, was made possible by many actors in the translocal field of protest, all of whom also provided me with great support beginning in January 2011 when I began this *yatra*. While it would be impossible to name everyone, I do thank all who have directly and indirectly contributed to this endeavor and apologize to those I inadvertently miss. I would, however, like to name and recognize some individuals and organizations that have been central to this effort.

Chief among them are three Gandhian leaders with whom I had the honor and privilege to engage in conversations and who died in the course of writing this book. Kantibhai Shah came from Bombay to Dharampur in the 1960s to work with the *adivasis*, co-founded the Sarvodaya Parivar Trust, and never left. He was seventy-nine when he died on April 29, 2012. An avid reader and writer, we spent many an evening at Pinvad discussing thinkers from Eric Fromm to Vinoba Bhave and topics ranging from science to spirituality to Bollywood films and music. Ilaben Pathak, an English professor, feminist leader, and founder of Ahmedabad Women's Action Group, died on January 10, 2014, at age eighty. Her generosity of spirit never wavered, and when I visited her as she was recovering from chemotherapy, she insisted on discussing how my book was coming along and if she could help. Chunnidada Vaidya, the Gandhian leader who joined the independent struggle as a teenager and then lived at the Sabarmati *ashram* in Ahmedabad, died on December 19, 2014, at age ninety-seven. A thin and frail ninety-four-year old when I first met him in 2011, his energy and enthusiasm for farmers' struggles could shame people a third his age. Together, these elders provided ongoing support and encouragement, warmth and laughter, and a wealth of historical and political analyses. To them, I am eternally grateful.

In the Nar-Par Adivasi Sangathan, I would like to thank Ansuyaben, Kashinathbhai, Rameshbhai, and Jayprakash. Ansuyaben, the song writer and singer for the Sangathan, not only talked to me for hours, but also invited me into her home and family and never let me leave her place without a care package, which at the last visit included groundnuts and rice grown on her farm so that I could savor the taste of her land when I was far away from it. Kashinathbhai, in his quiet and solemn way, was the one consistently concerned about how gender justice could be made an integral part of the various struggles in Dharampur and Gujarat. Rameshbhai not only discussed the struggle in minute detail, but also meticulously provided me with copies of all the documents. Jayprakash drove me countless times around the hilly terrain from Pinvad to Khadki and to the villages, educating me along the way about how life was changing for young *adivasi* men. At the Sarvodaya Parivar Trust, in addition to Kantibhai, Sujataben was the other staff member who was radicalized by the *adivasi* demands and who provided a wealth of insights into their work during and beyond the struggle. Ashaben and Virendrabhai, supporters of the trust from Valsad, were invaluable in providing me the context for the work of the trust and inviting me to various events organized by the trustees outside Dharampur, not to mention delicious home-cooked meals.

In the Mahuva movement, Kadviben and Dhanabhai took me under their wings and into their homes and fields and discussed the struggle at all hours of the day, while they were working in the fields in knee-deep water or cooking meals in the evening. Both had long histories of activism before the Mahuva movement and hence were key to understanding the larger and longer contexts for the struggle. The Utthan and Mahuva staff members Riteshbhai, Jeetendrabhai, and Ramudada all took time from their busy schedules to provide their insights and critique of the gendered aspects of the struggle. As the Mahatma of Mahuva, the leader of translocal and national struggles against dispossession, an elected member of the Gujarat assembly, and a practicing surgeon, Kanubhai never had a moment to spare. Yet he went about everything with the utmost calm and somehow managed to find time to talk to me at length and to make arrangements for me to meet with various activists across the *taluka*.

In Bhadreshwar, Bharatbhai Patel was an invaluable interlocutor, constantly challenging himself, MASS, SETU, Abhiyan, and others in the translocal and national fields. Ibrahimkaka, Ameenamasi, and Husseinbhai of MASS, as well as Bhadreshwar Setu staff Rakeshbhai, Usmanbhai, and Shymajibhai, took time to talk and provided logistical support. Sushmaben from KMVS was instrumental in establishing many of the women's movement organizations in the area and hence in my understanding of the gender

Acknowledgements xix

and social justice dynamics within Kutch. Reenaben from Ujjas elaborated on the ongoing gender justice work of MASS, SETU, and Ujjas.

Ahemdabad is the hub of the translocal field of protest in Gujarat and hence home to many long-time academics, activists, journalists, and other players who were key to understanding the history and ongoing political dynamics of the various struggles. Achyutbhai Yagnik, my mentor since 1985, as always, was invaluable in his insights and his generosity, not to mention his introductions to new actors in the field of protest. Similarly, Nafisaben Barot, the founder of Utthan; Maheshbhai Pandya of Paryavaran Mitra; and Sanjaybhai Dave of Charkha were key supporters. Thanks also to the colleagues at the Institute for Social Studies, Surat, with which I was affiliated during my research in India.

Beyond the three struggles and people associated with them, my year and work in India would not have been possible without the support of my extended family across Gujarat and Bombay. In Ahmedabad, Bakulamasi, Jayantmasa, Pranav, Mamta, Harsh, and Heth provided a home away from home. In Surat, Daksha and Jayesh were a constant source of support and facilitated my work and stay in all ways, including managing the myriad bureaucratic hurdles. In Valsad, Bakubhabhi, a fellow feminist, has been an advisor, inspiration, and a booster. In Mumbai, Rekha and Aayush have always provided a welcoming home. Words cannot convey my deep gratitude and love for my mummy, Nirmala Desai, and my brother, Alpesh Desai, whose unwavering support makes everything possible in India and underscores the loss of Nana, my dad, Kanu Desai.

Half a world away in the United States, my professional and personal debts are equally immense. The Fulbright Hays Faculty Research Abroad Fellowship, Award No. P019A100015, funded my research and stay in India from January 2011 to October 2011. Dean Teitelbaum's enthusiastic support enabled me to take time from my administrative responsibilities to embark on this research. Thanks are due to Elizabeth Mahan and her staff at UConn for shepherding my proposal through all its stages and to Betty Hansen, director of India Studies, and Cathy Schlund-Vials, director of Asian and Asian American Studies Institute, for their support throughout. I am especially grateful to Bandana Purkayastha, head of Sociology, for her constant support and encouragement during my time in India and since then that enabled me to complete this book. Thanks to Ordoitz Galilea for his prompt and careful attention to formatting the manuscript.

Over the years, I have been fortunate to be part of several intellectual and social communities, all of whom have been instrumental in shaping the scholar and person that I have become. My sisters in the Sociologists for Women in Society have been among the most important in that regard.

Micheline Ishay, Lisa Rosenthal, and Rachel Schurman have been there for me in more ways than I can count and for more decades than I want to. Anne Lambright, my writing buddy, thanks for our weekly accountability e-mails. We both did it! Guillermo Irizarry has been a dear friend, interlocutor, and listener. Gracias.

My family in the United States, you make it all possible. Thanks Estelle and Lester; Barbara, Mark, and Marie; and Roopa for your support and love. Ishan and Ilan, you are my joy and inspiration and fellow travelers in the struggles for social justice. To you I dedicate this book. Jeremy, for decades of unconditional love and friendship, not to mention editing and entertainment and celebrating me in moments of triumph and failure, thank you.

Glossary and abbreviations

abhiyan	campaign
adivasi	original inhabitants or indigenous groups
Adivasi Ekta Manch	Forum of Adivasi Unity
bachao	save
bandar	fishing piers
bandharo	small check dams
ben	sister, added after the first name of women to show respect
BSetu	Bhadreshwar SETU
bhai/bhau	brother, added after men's first names as a sign of respect
bicycle *yatra*	bike march
bunds	small dams
CRZ	coastal regulation zone
crore	monetary unit referring to 10,000,000
dada	paternal grandfather
dalit	literally oppressed; refers to those outside the caste system; "untouchables"
darbar	literally court, but used to refer to Rajput castes in Kutch
EIA	Environmental Impact Assessment
EMP	Environment Management Plan
gam or *gram*	village
gherao	Encircle
gram panchayat	elected village council
gram sabha	village council meeting
gram swaraj	village self-rule
gram swaraj samiti	village self-rule committee
harijan	literally children of God; moniker used by Mahatma Gandhi to refer to dalits

Glossary and abbreviations

jal	water
jamin	land
jaan	life
jan sunwai	public hearing
kaka	paternal uncle, often added to elder men's names to denote respect
Kanbi patel	a lower farming caste in Gujarat
Koli patel	a lower farming caste in Gujarat
Kshatriyas	warrior castes
Kutch Mahila Vikas Sangathan	Kutch Women's Development Organization
Kutch Navnirman Abhiyan	Campaign for the Reconstruction of Kutch
lakh	monetary unit referring to 100,000
lok samiti	people's committee
Macchimar Adhikar Sangharsh Samiti (MASS)	The Committee to Fight for Fishers' Rights
mahila panchayat	women's council/court
mahila sangathan	women's organization
mandal	group
mandir	temple
Mundra Heet Rakshak Manch	Forum for the Welfare of Mundra
Nar-Par Adivasi Sangathan	Adivasi Organization of Nar-Par Rivers
NFF	National Forum of Fishers
OBC	other backward caste, constitutional designation
OPG	Om Prakash Group
padyatra	literally pilgrimage by foot, a rally/march
pagadiya	foot fishers
panchayat	elected village council
Paryavaran Mitra	friend of the environment
Paryavarna Suraksha Samiti (PSS)	environment protection committee
Rabari	pastoral castes in Gujarat
SHG	self-help group
sarkar	government
sarpanch	elected head of the village council
satyagragh	truth force, protest
Setu	bridge

rath yatra	chariot rally
taluka	district subdivision
Ujjas	light
yatra	rally or march, literally pilgrimage
yatri	pilgrim, protestor

1 Legalism from below, translocal fields of protest, and gendered geographies

Jaan Denge Jamin Nahi![1] Gam ni Jamin Gamni Sarkar ni Nahi![2]
Chanting these slogans, hundreds of small farmers – women, men, and children – from the "Mahuva movement" carrying banners and flags and wearing bandanas that proclaim *Jal, Jamin, Jungle Bacho*[3] embark on a 350-kilometer *padyatra*[4] in Saurashtra, Gujarat, to protest the construction of Nirma Corporation's cement factory amidst the reservoirs that irrigate their fields.

Hundreds of kilometers to the northwest in Kutch, Gujarat, at an environmental public hearing, scores of fishers[5] from the *Machimar Adhikar Sangharsh Samiti* (Committee for the Struggle for Fishers' Rights, henceforth MASS) challenge the environment impact assessment of the power plant to be built by the Om Prakash Group, a private corporation.

In South Gujarat, *adivasi* (original inhabitants or indigenous peoples) youth from the *Nar Par Adivasi Sangathan* (Organization of Adivasis from Nar Par Rivers, henceforth Sangathan) stop four technicians subcontracted by the government to conduct field surveys in preparation for constructing dams and bring them in front of a spontaneously organized people's court to question them and educate them about the protest against the dams that would affect seventy-five villages and displace 14,832 people (see Figure 1.1).

These ongoing struggles of *adivasis*, fishers, and farmers have led to substantial victories against the state's neoliberal development project in one of the most developed states in the country.[6] With constant vigilance, the Sangathan in South Gujarat has prevented the state from undertaking the field surveys necessary to begin construction of the dams. The Mahuva movement in Saurashtra has been able to move the Supreme Court of India and the Green Tribunal of the national Ministry of Environment and Forest (MoEF) to order the dismantling of the cement factory. In Kutch, although MASS has been unable to stop the construction of the power plant,

2 Legalism from below

Figure 1.1 Map of Gujarat with the locations of the three struggles
Source: http://en.academic.ru/dic.nsf/enwiki/34268

it was successful in demanding a change in the plant's technology from a water-cooled system to an air-cooled one – the first time that a subaltern struggle has been able to achieve such a change. Although more expensive, this technology is less destructive of fishers' livelihoods and the environment. Gujarat is an important case to examine, as both in India and abroad it is a flashpoint around two issues, both attributed to its charismatic then chief minister, now prime minister, Narendra Modi: the success story of development and the massacre of Muslims in 2002. Yet, neither of these captures the failures of development or the successes of subaltern struggles. My book is a contribution in that direction.

In the current neoliberal conjuncture, why and how were these struggles able to succeed? What protest repertoire contributed to their success? How are these struggles gendered? What light do these struggles shed on development and democracy in India? What insights do they provide for scholarship on development, social movements, and gender? These are some of the questions that I address in this book. My main argument is that these movements succeeded because of the deepening of democracy in India, albeit in tandem with the increasing coercive powers of the state. But they also demonstrate the ways in which gender remains a challenge for the state and subaltern movements, as well as for social theory, and call into question the extent of democratic deepening.

The ongoing "reinvention" of state–society relations in post-colonial India, Corbridge and Harris (2000) argued, is being shaped by contradictory political processes of "elite revolts" against state intervention and subaltern politics that demand a state response to their oppression and exclusion from development. Subaltern politics, beginning in the late 1960s, contributed to this in two ways. First, they shaped the state's legal architecture, sometimes directly – for example, through mobilization that resulted in the Right to Information Act of 2005 – and at other times indirectly, such as the public interest litigation initiated by the Supreme Court in the 1980s in the aftermath of the Emergency following the various subaltern movements of the 1960s. Similarly, the Panchayati Raj Act of 1993 was an effort to respond to growing subaltern frustrations and mobilizations.

All these legal changes provided opportunities for "legalism from below," key to the success of all three struggles. Defined by Eckert (2006: 45) as the ways in which subaltern groups use "legal terms against the transgressions of law by state agents and other bodies of governmental authority," legalism from below has become a dominant part of the contemporary protest repertoire of many subaltern social movements in India. From gaining information via the Right to Information Act, to participating in environmental public hearings and filing public interest litigation, the struggles engage in a form of "rightful resistance" (O'Brien and Li 2006). Thus, contrary to the "legal fetishism" (Comaroff and Comaroff 2009) of the neoliberal age, the collective and critical nature of legalisms from below transforms law from abstractions to what Mulqueen and Tatryn (2012) call "law as ontology," in the process challenging and extending the very conception of legal categories.

Second, earlier subaltern politics, specifically the *Nav Nirman* (reconstruction) movement and *Narmada Bachao Andolan* (Struggle to Save the Narmada, henceforth NBA) in Gujarat,[7] also contributed to what I call a *translocal field of protest*, composed of ongoing relationships among multiple local fields of protest. From the beginning, each struggle was constituted by and contributed to this translocal field. Based on a call of *vikas joyeh, vinash nahi* (we want development, not destruction),[8] the struggles not only supported each other, but also engaged in more ongoing work of mobilizing and sharing collective, critical practices, thus creating and sustaining a translocal field of protest.

Many of the same players, such as cause lawyers, journalists, academics, activists, and advocates, were active in the three struggles, operating in the same arenas such as the courts, the streets, nongovernmental organizations

(NGOs), research centers, and subaltern communities (Jasper 2013). Thus neoliberalism has not only generated the dispossession of subaltern groups, but also consolidated linkages among movement actors. These linkages are facilitated not only because of newer technologies, but also by understanding the struggles as a response to the same neoliberal logic, which must be countered by articulating with other struggles. These translocal solidarities were also crucial to their success. The three struggles not only protested their dispossession from their land and loss of livelihood, but also revived Gandhi's *gram swaraj* (village self-rule) as a homegrown alternative model of development through collective dialogues, workshops, and mobilizations.

These struggles thus challenge several arguments about subaltern protests against development. One, articulated by Levien (2013), among others, sees the subaltern politics of dispossession, or land wars, as ad hoc, single issue, and occurring in an organizational void. The other suggests that subaltern protests represent a form of neoliberal governmentality, and rights-based claims are an indication of shrinking space for transformative politics (e.g., Chatterjee 2010; Nielsen 2011; Ray and Katzenstein 2005). Finally, some analysts see subaltern protests as alternatives to development that are autonomous from the state and based on indigenous cosmovisions (e.g., Escobar 2008).

Yet, these struggles also reveal what I call a *gendered geography of struggle*. Influenced by nearly four decades of women's movements and women's empowerment projects of the state, subaltern women are active in large numbers in all three struggles. But they are visible and audible in only some spaces of the struggles and in those sometimes more so than subaltern men. Contrary to expectations, they appear most prominently in the public spaces of *yatras* (marches) and *jan sunwais* (public hearings) or meetings with public officials, but are marginalized in the private, decision-making spaces of the struggles. Furthermore, each struggle engages in a gender division of political labor, wherein mobilizing women and addressing women's issues are done by women's movement organizations (WMOs) in the area and not within the struggle.

Nonetheless, these struggles, along with many others currently underway in Gujarat and across the country, challenge the monolithic narrative of vibrant Gujarat and India Shining promoted by Prime Minister Modi and embraced by the elite and middle classes, even as they demonstrate the challenges to the deepening of development and democracy.

State, social movements, and democracy in India

Most scholars of post-colonial India agree that nation building was monopolized by the dominant classes to serve their interests (e.g., Chatterjee

1993; Frankel 2005; Kaviraj 1997). They also agree that today, however, the political terrain is undergoing significant changes (e.g., Corbridge and Harris 2000; Frankel 2005; Frankel and Rao 1990; Nigam and Menon 2007; Nilsen 2010). One indicator of these changes is the subaltern movements that initially emerged in full force across many parts of India beginning in the 1960s.

Termed alternatively as the new social movements (Omvedt 1993) or nonparty political formations (Kothari 1984), these movements sought recognition of themselves and their issues that went beyond those that either the Congress or the left parties had acknowledged, such as caste, gender, and the environment. Beyond recognition, they also sought redistribution and inclusion in the political process that only sought their vote every election cycle but did not include them as citizens in any meaningful way and delivered little of what was promised at election times (Baviskar 1995; Guha 1989; Nilsen 2010; Ray and Katzenstein 2005). Although these movements did go through a period of abeyance in the 1990s, they have reemerged across the country in response to the dispossession entailed in the liberalizing policies. Moreover, although many are focused on immediate issues of loss of land and livelihood, some are also engaged in more ongoing political work that has the potential for radical possibilities.

Another element of the changing political terrain is the rise of *dalit* and lower-caste political parties, or the "silent revolution," especially in Northern India (Jaffrelot 2003; Witsoe 2013; Yadav 2000) but also in parts of Southern India (e.g., Subramanian 2009). For the first time since independence, these parties have been able to wrest political power from the Congress party at the state levels, though this has not led to economic and political empowerment of subaltern groups in these states. Rather, as Witsoe (2013) shows, in Bihar the lower-caste parties reproduced the governance strategies of the upper castes, which not only continued corruption on a massive scale, but also a movement away from development. Additionally, there have been armed Maoist struggles in the resource-rich "red belt" across the center of the country (Mukherjee 2012; Shah 2010).

What scholars and analysts debate, as Nilsen (2012) notes, is the nature of the relationship between the subaltern social movements and the state, their ability to empower themselves through state development projects, and how this might contribute to the deepening of democracy in India. Nilsen (2012) characterizes these disagreements as anti-statist and state-centric. The anti-statists, such as Chatterjee (1993) and Kaviraj (1997), argue that the state still remains in the control of the dominant groups and through a "passive revolution" involving control of economic resources, they have ensured that development benefits them primarily and, to some extent, the middle classes, but very little reaches the subaltern classes. Moreover, both

6 Legalism from below

the state and dominant groups continue to use coercive power to control subaltern groups, as evident in the suppression of Maoist insurgencies, belying any deepening of democracy. Thus, the subaltern social movements, these critics contend, have failed to dismantle the hold of the dominant groups and to advance their interests.

The state-centric scholars (e.g., Corbridge and Harris 2000; Desai 2007; Heller 1999; Kohli 1987), by contrast, argue that subaltern movements, sometimes with the help of left political parties in states like Kerala and West Bengal, have been able to access the state, and it might be their only avenue to economic and political empowerment. Scholars such as Gupta (2012), Sharma (2008), and Subramanian (2009) have shown how subaltern groups at the local level are able to use rights-based claims to access the state successfully. Moving beyond this binary, Nilsen (2012) proposes a framework that looks at the micro-politics of state–society relations in the context of the changing nature of the political economy. Thus, following Jessop (2008), he argues that the extent to which subaltern movements have been able to expand and enhance their economic and political power is shaped both by structural constraints and conjunctural opportunities. Based on his analysis of the *Narmada Bachao Andolan*, he argues that the failure to prevent the construction of the dams demonstrates the limit of the subaltern movements' ability to enlist state power in their interest and the need for oppositional or counter-hegemonic projects to ensure their emancipation and social transformation.

In analyzing the relationship between the state, social movements, and democracy, most of the previously mentioned scholars have not addressed the place of gender, although the "women's question," has been debated vigorously by feminist scholars, for example, Jayawardena (1986), Mazumdar (1985), Menon (1999), and Sangari and Vaid (1989). They have argued that with the exception of personal laws, the elite considered the women's question solved at independence. The efforts of the nationalist women's movement had resulted in suffrage and the constitutional guarantee of social, economic, and political equality (e.g., Kumar 1993). Personal laws, that is, laws relating to marriage, divorce, inheritance, and child custody, were to be determined according to the customary laws of each religion. Although this was seen as an effort in the bloody aftermath of partition to quell religious fervor, it meant that women were not incorporated as equal citizens at independence. It was up to each religious community to reform its laws to guarantee equality, and even today there is no uniform civil code to address these issues.

Such compromised rights for women were also evident in the ways in which educated women from the dominant groups were incorporated in the state bureaucracy, and to some extent in the political parties, but for the majority of subaltern women, those constitutional rights meant very little. It was in the context of the subaltern politics of the 1960s and the "Towards Equality" report of the national government in 1974 – in preparation for the United Nations First World Conference on Women – that "the women's question" reemerged for the state and in social movements. Until then, left parties were among the main actors who focused on subaltern women. In response to the United Nation's International Women's Year in 1975, followed by the International Women's Decade from 1975–1985, and a decade later the Women's World Conference in Beijing, the Indian state developed a gender equality regime in keeping with the global gender equality regime (e.g., Desai 2008; Kardam 2004; Snyder 2006).

This gender equality regime has included the creation of a women's policy machinery, that is, ministries and commissions and policies and programs to empower women and to mainstream gender (e.g., Banaszak, Beckwith, and Rucht 2003; Ferree and Tripp 2006; McBride and Mazur 2010). In most of these gender projects, gender is synonymous with women; men are rarely addressed. Moreover, women are implicitly or explicitly seen as victims of patriarchal cultures who need to be empowered through educational, economic, and political strategies (e.g., Menon 2009; Sinha 2012). The gendered, particularly masculine, nature of state structures, procedures, and discourses that disadvantage most women, and subaltern men, is not taken into consideration.

Hence, despite such state gender projects of women's empowerment, there has not been a substantive change in the lives of most women in India or around the world. Studies on women's policy machineries show that these are mostly underfunded and marginalized and have not affected the gendered organization and culture of state bureaucracies (e.g., Kardam 2004; McBride and Mazur 2010; Tripp, Casimiro, Kwesiga, and Mungwa 2009). Similarly, gender mainstreaming has been understood variously and thus implemented haphazardly and has failed to address the relational aspects of gendered structures and organizational culture (e.g., IFJP 2005; Walby 2005). The coincidence of states' gender projects with the rise of neoliberalism has further circumscribed their strategies to those based on a market calculus, which empower women only as economic agents and political managers rather than as citizens with rights (e.g., Basu 2010; Menon 2009; Sharma 2011).

Within subaltern movements, scholar activists such as Sen (1990) argued that not only was there "space within the struggle" for women, but there was also a "struggle within the struggle" for women's issues. But other women activists saw women and women's issues subordinated to class issues and delegated to women activists – a gendered division of political labor (e.g., Gandhi and Shah 1992). In keeping with the call for participatory democracy and non-party affiliation in subaltern movements of the time, women activists called for an autonomous women's movement that would be autonomous from political parties and movements and that would highlight women's issues, including the gendered nature of class and caste conflicts. Unlike the anti-statist and state-centric perspectives, feminists of the autonomous movements have always argued for working with, against, and through the state as a necessary part of a multi-pronged approach to democratizing society (e.g., Basu 1992, Gandhi and Shah 1992, Kumar 1993, Menon 2004).

A similar multi-pronged repertoire is evident in the subaltern struggles that are the focus of this book.

Legalism from below: beyond weapons of the weak and subaltern legal pluralism to law as social movement

Although laws, directly or indirectly, have always played a part in subaltern struggles, in the neoliberal age of "legal fetishism" (Comaroff and Comaroff 2009), they have star billing. Defined as legalism from below,[9] this subaltern legal engagement has been theorized either as instrumental or representing a subaltern cosmopolitan legality defined by legal pluralism. Scholars making the former argument (e.g., Eckert 2006; Merry 2006), often write in relation to human rights struggles in national and international contexts. Eckert (2006) argues that the "use of law" now "complements or replaces" other kinds of resistances, such as protests, and has become "the weapon of the weak." Furthermore, they argue, the active and creative ways in which the poor engage the law has potential for the law to be an emancipatory instrument rather than one that only reproduces hegemony. Eckert (2006), for example, notes that although it might be difficult to assess the success of legalism from below, she agrees with Banerjee (1999: 6 cited in Eckert 2006: 63) that it presents a "genuinely philosophical grasp of democratic principles and good governance and ideas about rights and citizenship among rural voters."

Similarly, Meszaros (2013) notes that social movements in Brazil are not just using the law to make the state accountable, but are drivers of new legal interpretations and shapers of substantive democracy. O'Brien and Li (2006) make a similar case for rightful resistance in China, which they argue is a result of state building as well as the spread of participatory ideologies rooted in notions of equality, rights, and rule of law. Rightful resistance, however, is episodic and does not always result in more ongoing protests. These analysts all note, however, that this is an uneven process and not always successful because of entrenched power interests, but nevertheless it represents a radical shift in legal activism by subaltern groups.

Thus, Eckert (2006) argues that this use of the law by subaltern groups represents an acceptance of a universal legal framework (or order) that even as it is contested and reinterpreted is also used as the basis for making claims. This contrasts with the centrality of legal pluralism in subaltern struggles, extensively theorized by Santos (e.g., 2002, and Santos and Rodriguez-Garavita 2005), among others. Legal pluralism is a multiplicity of legal orders that co-exist within the same political and social territory. Although it also existed in medieval Europe, today it is often associated with countries of the Global South, where it is assumed to be the result of colonization. Thus, in colonial contexts two legal orders co-existed: that of the colonial state in matters economic and political, and that of the native, religious, and/or customary for familial and social affairs. In reality, the multiple legal orders were never so circumscribed but inserted themselves in all domains. And in India, as elsewhere, legal pluralism did not emerge with colonialism. It existed in various forms in pre-colonial state polities as well.

Santos (2002) defined legal plurality primarily in opposition to Western, liberal legal theory, which he argued was both uniform and state centered and in which there was no room for other legal orders. This hegemonic legality, according to him, does not recognize the subaltern and hence in its very conception has limited potential for emancipatory possibilities. Legal pluralism, by contrast, by not being state centric and challenging its hegemony, has more emancipatory possibilities. I have argued (Desai 2009) that the existence of different legalities is not always emancipatory but depends on the nature of legal orders, the actors who invoke them, and the purposes for which they do so. Thus, in the case of India, I showed that religious personal laws reflected regulatory rather than emancipatory practices, though the latter were not precluded as evidenced by the ways in which women's groups have used them for gender justice.

Similarly, Sieder and McNeish (2012) argue that the question is not about the desirability of legal pluralism, as it exists in many countries in the Global South, but rather how it affects gender justice in the context of development. Since non-state legalities are not always enforceable, it is not always clear whether they are a resource or a liability for women in particular and subaltern groups in general. Thus, they argue that regimes of governance, as well as the gender projects of different actors, shape the potential of legal pluralities for emancipatory politics.

In a different vein, Mulqueen and Tataryn (2012) argue for law as the "coming together of people in common social movements, i.e., law as social movement" (Mulqueen and Tataryn 2012: 292). Based on their analysis of the Occupy Wall Street movement, they highlight the not-always-successful negotiation of a democratic legality within the various community structures that emerged in response to the protest. Their claim is "that it is worthwhile recognising law and community in constant movement – actively defining and defying law (Mulqueen and Tataryn 2012: 296). Blecher (2008), in a similar vein, argues that:

> ... both social movements and "law in movement" take (and must take) as their aim the permanent "constitutional act" necessary to de- and re-construct the parameters of the common, of justice, wealth, truth, etc. This includes the potential re-invention of the entire organisational and decisional set-up, including new common institutions and respective governance procedures, which will obviously also transform the very movement itself.
>
> (Blecher 2008: 302)

Thus, Mulqueen and Tatryn and Blecher, following Paine's (1992) conception of law as an expression of the will of the community, focus on a constant redefinition of the legal field by people to meet their common aspirations, rather than relationships among static legal orders.

In response to such theorizations, Esteva (2007), among others, has argued for a multi-tiered legal plurality that both engages the state legality (order) and articulates it with legal pluralism – what Santos (2002) has defined as interlegality. Esteva's analysis is based on the practices of the Popular Assembly of the Peoples of Oxaca (APPO), Mexico. A convergence of various labor, peasant, feminist, cultural, indigenous, environmental, urban, and regional groups – what he calls a movement of movements – the APPO emerged in response to the state repression of a teachers' union. Its multi-tiered democratic practices begin with using state laws to counter corruption and fraud that hamper formal legal processes so that they might respond better to the needs of subaltern groups; it introduces greater participatory democratic processes such as local budgeting, plebiscites, and social oversight of administrative processes; and finally, it anchors the previous two practices in a local, community-based, grassroots radical democracy derived from traditions of indigenous communities.

The three struggles in Gujarat similarly demonstrate a multi-tiered legal plurality. Each has used legalism from below as a weapon of the weak to challenge the state and corporations as rightful resistance, but each has also gone beyond that to engage in participatory, democratic processes in their cooperatives and producer companies, *gram panchayat* (village council) trainings, and formulation of alternative legal practices such as *mahila panchayats* (women's courts) to deal with violence within their communities, and spontaneous people's courts to make outsiders accountable to the community. This legalism from below was facilitated by and through the translocal field of protest and solidarities.

Translocal field of protest and translocal solidarities

Drawing upon Bourdieu, Raka Ray (1999: 7) defined the political field as

> the state, political parties, and social movements organizations, who are connected to each other in both friendly and antagonistic ways, some of whose elements are more powerful than others, and all of whom are tied together by a particular culture.

The critical or oppositional elements in such a political field constitute the field of protest, which "consists of groups and networks that oppose those who have power in the formal political arena and may or may not share the logic of politics in the larger political field, although they are constrained by it" (Ray 1999: 8).

Although Ray defined the field of protest, most of her analytical framework focused on characterizing the political field itself. Specifically, she characterized political fields in terms of their political culture – either homogenous or heterogeneous – and concentration of power, either concentrated or dispersed. I elaborate on Ray's field of protest by providing it a spatial dimension and define a translocal field of protest as relationships among multiple, local fields of protest. Such a spatial dimension is evident in Bourdieu's observation that "[t]he limits of the field are situated at the point where the effects of the field cease" (cited in Ray 1999: 10).

My usage of translocal charts a different scale, but is conceptually similar to its common use in the transnational literature. Appadurai (1996), Featherstone (2008), and McFarlane (2009), among others, defined the translocal to highlight the importance of place, not as a bounded entity but one produced via social relations, to people's identities and politics even as they moved across transnational borders. I share a similar relational understanding of place and its importance in people's lives and politics, but the "trans" in my case is not across national borders but within a region in a nation, though it does not have to be restricted to it.

The translocal field of protest is the dynamic relationships among movement actors of various local fields of protest. Solidarity as "mutuality, accountability, and recognition of common interests" (Mohanty 2003: 7) is the basis of these relationships. The translocal field of protest for the struggles in this book is constituted by the relationships among social movements, non-governmental organizations (NGOs), advocates, academics, journalists, and supporters in the local fields of protest in Dharampur/Valsad (for the Sangathan), Kutch (for MASS), Mahuva (for the Mahuva movement), and Ahmedabad, which served as a node for the translocal field of protest.

A translocal field of protest is internally differentiated by movements such as the women's movements, the environmental movements, Gandhian NGOs, and farmers' movements, among others, each of which have relations with other such movements across regional, national, and transnational scales. Each of the struggles had relationships with several of these movements. Given the complexity of the field, it is also a site of contested power relations between and among actors. As such, Ray's characterization of the political field along dimensions of political culture and distribution of power also applies to the translocal field of protest. Thus, a homogenous political culture with concentration of power would mean that there is less toleration of diversity and the dominant groups within the field are more dominant. Similarly, a heterogeneous political culture in a dispersed field would mean greater diversity of organizations and ideologies. In Gujarat, the translocal field of protest has a heterogeneous political culture and is fragmented with a diversity of organizations and ideologies.

The major ways in which the translocal field of protest facilitated each of the struggles was by providing a repertoire or tool kit from which activists drew (Martin 2013, Tilly 2008); professional resources for legalism from below and policy advocacy; material and logistical support, as well as participation in *yatras* and other protest activities; and in developing pre-figurative politics, such as collective dialogues, self-help groups, and knowledge practices such as "ground truthing." Thus, like McFarlane's (2009) concept of translocal assemblages, the translocal field is not just a spatial category or resultant formation, but signifies doing, performance, and events. The relationships among actors in this field are one of the factors that shape the gendered geographies of the struggles.

Gendered geographies of struggle

The scholarship on gender and social movements highlights the mutually constitutive relationship between them. The concept of gender regime, that is, the gendered structures, procedures, and discourses of the state and other institutions, has been used to explain variation in the political and cultural opportunities for protest, as well as the internal dynamics of movements (Kuumba 2001, Taylor 1999; Whittier 2007; Yulia 2010). Most of this scholarship has emerged from analyzing women's movements.

Feminist scholars, however, have also been demonstrating the multiple ways in which the internal dynamics of mixed-gender movements are gendered (e.g., Gandhi and Shah 1992, Jayawardena 1986, Kumar 1993, Maier and Lebon 2010, Omvedt 1993, Tripp, Casimiro, Kwesiga, and Mungwa 2009). In nationalist, revolutionary, and other social movements, scholars have observed two patterns. First, traditional gender roles are replicated within movements, where women do the "domestic" work of the movement or work on women's issues, while men do the political work. For example, in Latin America and India, women active in the left movements experienced the subordination of women's issues to those of class and caste and the relegation of those issues to women activists. It was frustration with these experiences that led women to organize autonomous feminist movements (e.g., Gandhi and Shah 1992; Maier and Lebon 2010). Similarly, in the case of the new left and civil rights movement in the United States, it was the confining of women to housekeeping work that led many to question their role in the movements and start the second wave of the women's movements (e.g., Evans 1980).

Second, women are marginalized in terms of representation and leadership. For example, Robnett (2000) showed how black women were prevented by the gender hierarchy of black churches and the civil rights movement from taking on formal leadership positions. In response, they developed their own informal, or "bridge," leadership, which was key to mobilization and solidarity within the civil rights movement. More recently, Conway (2013) and Eschle and Maiguashca (2010) found a similar marginality of women and feminism at the World Social Forum. Conway argues that despite the contributions of the various feminist movements to the project of global justice, they remain under-recognized and marginalized in leadership. Eschle and Maiguashca (2010) use the metaphor of a skeleton woman to evoke the shadowy presence of feminist movements at the World Social Forum and their efforts for visibility, voice, and influence.

Thus, most scholarship has focused on the importance of gender regimes to explain the reproduction of gender inequalities in mixed-gender movements. But in the past four decades the systemic efforts of the women's movements to challenge patriarchal gender regimes and to articulate the global gender equality regime via the United Nations have also resulted in gender projects for women's empowerment. And while much has been written on the fragmentation, institutionalization, and NGO-ization of women's movements, especially in the current neoliberal moment (e.g., Alvarez 2009; Basu 2010, Moghadam 2012, Walby 2013), it has not resulted in dismantling either the state or the feminist gender projects. Rather, as Horn (2013) notes, women' rights and gender justice have now become part of various mixed-gender movements around social justice. And these women's empowerment projects, I argue, also affect gender dynamics in mixed-gender movements.

14 *Legalism from below*

In India, as noted earlier, the contemporary women's movements emerged in the early 1970s from subaltern movements around issues of livelihood and land (e.g., Gandhi and Shah 1992; Kumar 1993; Omvedt 1993). Autonomous women's movements emerged in the early 1980s in response to the marginalization of women's issues in these movements. And although the autonomous groups were primarily based in the urban areas and mobilized against issues of violence against women, many continued to bring these issues and others to subaltern women in rural areas.

Among such groups were *Utthan* in Ahmedabad, Gujarat, which has a branch in Mahuva, and Kutch *Mahila Vikas* in Kutch (Kutch Women's Development), which has launched several WMOs in MASS's field of protest. These autonomous groups, through their branches in rural areas, work on an ongoing basis with rural women. It was through such projects of the autonomous women's movement that subaltern women in this study became politicized. Their activism has included ongoing training through workshops and gatherings and engaging with regional feminist issues and networks. Later, they also took advantage of the state's reservation of 33% of seats for women in local governance and the self-help groups, launched to raise women's consciousness and also as savings groups. Thus, it is because of such women's empowerment projects that subaltern women appear in contemporary subaltern movements, albeit only in certain spaces resulting in a *gendered geography of struggle*.

By gendered geography of struggle, I mean the place of women and men in movement spaces, that is, where, when, and how women and men are visible and audible. Movements, I argue, are multi-sited, including local spaces such as the house of a village elder or an NGO office which serves as a gathering place and where routine activism such as meetings, discussions, and planning take place; the space of protest rallies and marches, which themselves are multi-leveled, as I discuss in Chapter 4; and the spaces of convergence and encounter where activists of different movements meet and which are often in distant towns and regions. I argue that contrary to gender norms, in the three struggles in this book, subaltern women are visible and audible in the public spaces of the struggle such as the marches and rallies and meetings with public officials, but not in the private spaces such as the office or in translocal encounters. Where they are visible in these more routine and private spaces is within WMOs in the area.

Thus, the gendered geography of struggle also extends outside each struggle to the local and translocal field of protest. In this second spatial organization, women's organizations in the region are responsible for mobilizing women for the struggle, but addressing women's issues outside the struggles. Each struggle had a different pattern of engagement with WMOs in their local field of protest. Within the Sangathan, there was no ongoing relationship with any specific WMO and *adivasi* women had to assert themselves to be included in the internal spaces of the struggle. *Adivasi* women's self-assertion was shaped both by their cultural histories of greater freedom and mobility, and also by their prior collective organizing around livelihood projects. The Mahuva movement had close ties with a WMO in their local field of protest and with feminist leaders in the translocal field of protest, and women's issues were "outsourced" to them and seldom addressed within the struggle. Even when such issues were raised within the struggle, it was not seen as the place to address them. In MASS there was "ongoing engagement" with several WMOs in their local and translocal field of protest, ensuring that the struggle attempted, not always successfully, to incorporate women in all spaces within the struggle and to address gender justice within the struggle.

What these patterns reveal is that although there are spaces, albeit outside the struggle, for subaltern women to address gender issues, there are no such spaces for subaltern men. This sometimes leads to situations whereby the visibility of subaltern women results in derision and violence against them by subaltern men. In the local field of protest of the Mahuva movement and MASS, women's organizations are making some attempts to include subaltern men in addressing gender issues. These different patterns of engagement, I argue, are a result of the political commitments of what I call the *movement anchors* of each struggle.

Movement anchors may be pre-existing NGOs or more loosely structured entities or groups of political leaders and activists who are central to each struggle. Their contributions range from providing leadership to initiating legal action on behalf of subaltern groups, to coordinating collective action and advocating on their behalf, to providing space and other resources to the struggle. The anchor for the Sangathan is the *Sarvodaya* (welfare of all) *Parivar* (family) Trust, a Gandhian NGO supported by private donations that has worked for over forty years in the *adivasi* villages providing subsidized grain and roof tiles as well as health and education facilities. Its focus has thus been on "constructive" work, and there is no specific focus on gender.

The movement anchor for the Mahuva movement comprises four political leaders: Kanu*bhai*[10] Kalsaria, their elected state representative until 2012; Sanatbhai Mehta, a Congress leader and erstwhile finance minister of the state; until her death in January 2014, feminist activist Ila*ben* Pathak; and until his death in December 2014, veteran Gandhian activist Chunni*dada* Vaidya. The latter two were members of an informally structured entity called the *Gujarat Lok Samiti* (People's Committee) initiated by Chunnidada. It had no formal structure or membership, but was used to initiate dialogue and collective action. Although the political leaders seldom questioned the gendered geography beyond ensuring women's participation, the presence of Ilaben meant that women's issues were raised in the struggle, even if they were rarely addressed.

Finally, the movement anchor for MASS was Bhadreshwar SETU, an NGO established by a network of NGOs to initially address issues of rehabilitation following two hurricanes and an earthquake but which grew over time into a community resource center focused on empowering local communities. From the beginning, Bhadreshwar SETU focused on organizing women and youth in developing self-governing collectives to address issues faced in the communities. Toward this, they also worked actively with WMOs in their local and translocal field of protest. Thus, gender justice was central to the work of Bhadreshwar SETU and hence to MASS.

How these different movement anchors and their local and translocal fields of protests shaped the struggles and their gendered geographies is the focus of the book.

The three struggles

When I went to Gujarat in January 2011, my aim was to study how women's and environmental movements and NGOs in the state were responding to the dispossession of subaltern groups in the rapid development of the state. Such dispossession had been the focus of much popular and academic writing in India for the past decade. Most of the militant Maoist protests by subaltern groups against this dispossession had been in other parts of India, and I was not aware of the three struggles when I landed in Ahmedabad. It was in meetings with several scholars and activists that I learned of the upcoming *padyatra* of the Mahuva movement and about MASS. And it was during the *padyatra* that I learned of the struggle in South Gujarat. Although unaware of these struggles, I have been involved with movement communities in Gujarat since the mid-1980s and have long-term relationships with activists, journalists, and scholars in the region, which facilitated my access to these struggles.

Fortuitously, each of the three struggles mobilized a different subaltern group (*adivasis*, lower-caste farmers, and Muslim fishers), located in three different regions of Gujarat (Saurashtra, Kutch, and South Gujarat), around three different kinds of dispossession, yet all three were a product of the same development logic providing an opportunity for comparative analysis. Furthermore, each of the struggles was anchored by a movement organization with different histories and political commitments, allowing another axis of comparison. Despite this variability, what was common to all three struggles was the large participation of women that allowed me to address the gendered nature of the struggles.

The three struggles are in three regions of Gujarat separated by hundreds of kilometers. Two of these regions, Saurashtra and Kutch, were independent political and administrative entities during the colonial period and became part of Gujarat only in 1960. They have a distinct political and social culture, not the least because of their location on peninsular Gujarat. Yet, in all three struggles, I encountered some of the same individual actors, both subaltern and non-subaltern. Hence, I began to see early on the importance of what I came to call the translocal field of protest.

During and after my field research there were several other mobilizations against "land wars" in many parts of Gujarat. For example, currently there is a struggle against the *Mithi Virdi* nuclear power plant; against Tata's Nano car plant in Sanand, which had been ousted from West Bengal; and against the Special Investment Region (SIR) stretching hundreds of kilometers from northern to southern Gujarat. I was unable, for reasons of time and resources, to follow these and other emerging struggles. But they all illustrate the active citizenship of subaltern groups and the dynamism of the translocal field of protest in Gujarat.

Notes on methodology

I conducted two seasons of field research: the first from January to November 2011, and the second from October to November 2013. My field research involved commuting between the sites of the three struggles. I spent roughly three months in the villages in each site. I also spent several weeks in Ahmedabad, the largest city and the node of the translocal field of protest and close to the state capital of Gandhinagar.

During my time in the villages, I "observed participation" (Kaminski 2004) and participated in the daily and movement activities of subaltern activists and participants. I conducted semi-structured and informal interviews. I interviewed movement participants, subaltern and non-subaltern activists, local government officials, and journalists. In total, I conducted sixty semi-structured interviews and numerous informal interviews in my first season and another twenty in my second season. Together, I interviewed forty-three men and thirty-seven women. The slight gender disparity reflects the disparity among the activists and other professionals. The interviews lasted from twenty minutes to two hours, and I interviewed several activists multiple times.

Most of the interviews were conducted in Gujarati. Some, about ten, were conducted in a mix of English and Gujarati. These were primarily with officials and academics. I transcribed all the interviews and translated the Gujarati into English. With the exception of some state officials, most people I interviewed did so on record and were happy to be identified by their real names. Hence, in general I have identified people by name, except when writing about sensitive issues. When referring to people, I have used the respectful Gujarati usage of referring to women by their first names followed by the term *ben*, sister, and for men the term *bhai*, for brother. For a few elderly activists, I have used the kinship term for uncle, *kaka*; maternal aunt, *masi*; and paternal grandfather, *dada*.

Additionally, I participated in various protest activities. I walked for five days in the *padyatra* of the Mahuva movement, walking six to eight hours each day, singing, resting, and sharing meals with the protestors. I had informal conversations with many of them over several days. Such intensive participation builds a level of camaraderie and rapport that would otherwise take weeks. I also participated for two days in the bicycle *yatra* and attended numerous meetings, collective dialogues, training sessions, and workshops. I kept detailed field notes following each of the sessions. I also collected primary documents produced by the movement, as well as newspaper, magazine, and newsletter accounts about the struggles and state documents related to the issues. I coded the transcripts, field notes, and documentary sources for themes that emerged and developed my analysis around them.

As extensive feminist, social movement, and post-colonial literatures attest, writing about subaltern struggles in India from a location in the US academy is fraught with contradictions. But as Spivak (2012) reminds us, this calls for an ethic of responsibility to work towards a project of transformation even as our current privilege enmeshes us in reproducing power inequalities. As Desai, Bouchard, and Detournay (2010: 60–61) note:

> ... all knowledge production is predicated upon epistemic violence and is a form of stealing and demands an explicit ethic of acknowledging and emphasizing that knowledge production is based on and shaped by unequal power relations. Recognizing such thievery is a way of furthering responsibility as a persistent question without resolution.

Feminists and other scholar-activists use several strategies to work towards such responsibility, ranging from individual strategies of "immediate reciprocity" (Gillan and Pickerill 2012), experimenting with forms of writing, and self-reflexivity, to more collective ones based on "general reciprocity."

Following what Conway (2013) calls moving forward questioning, I see the struggles as narratives that contribute to theoretical and political thinking and not as Southern data to be mined for Northern theory (e.g., Connell 2011, Santos 2014). Hence, I study them with the same degree of critical engagement as other articulations, contributing to what Santos (2014) has called an ecology of knowledges. In the months that I spent with the *adivasis*, farmers, fishers, and others involved in the struggles, I saw myself as one of many interlocutors with a long-term commitment to movements for social justice. Hence, I shared my analysis with several of the players in each struggle.

Chapter outline

Following this introduction, in Chapter 2 I present the Indian and Gujarati contexts that shape these struggles. I show that these three struggles, along with a host of others currently underway in Gujarat and India, are a result of the dispossession resulting from the state's neoliberal development model and the deepening of democracy evident in the (1) legal architecture of public interest litigation initiated by the Supreme Court, and the Panchayati Raj Act of 1993 and its impact on other legislations, including the newly legislated Right to Information Act (RTI) of 2005; (2) the state's movement between a privatizing and a redistributive mode (e.g., Sharma 2008); and (3) the consolidation of the social movement and NGO fields of force over the past four decades that have radicalized subaltern subjectivities and are contributing to a project of transformation.

In Chapter 3 I examine the Nar-Par Adivasi Sangathan's six-year struggle to prevent the construction of dams on local rivers in the context of their ongoing histories of exploitation and resistance. I show how the *adivasi* community radicalized their movement anchor, the Sarvodaya Parivar Trust – which had been working in the area for four decades around issues of health, education, housing, and livelihood assistance – to engage in protest. Through translocal solidarities with other environmental activists, they used the RTI to file petitions and get information that enabled them to mobilize consensus among the seventy-five villages to be affected by the dams and, to date, prevent the construction of the dams. I also show how the political commitment of the trust and the sporadic nature of relationships between the trust and WMOs in the local and translocal field of protest meant that the gendered geography of the struggle was challenged only by the *adivasi* women themselves.

Chapter 4 illuminates the dynamics of the Mahuva movement. After the *Narmada Bachao Andolan*, some analysts in Gujarat consider it the most successful subaltern movement against development in Gujarat. I demonstrate the convergence of various factors that enabled farmers in Mahuva to challenge corporate capital. Important to its success are the specifics of the farmers' claim that the factory was being built in irrigated farmland that is protected by environmental legislation, the militancy of the subaltern farmers who are supporters of the ruling Bharatiya Janata Party (BJP), the commitment of their state legislator who led the struggle and even resigned from the ruling party, and the support of established Gandhian and feminist leaders and cause lawyers from the translocal field of protest. I also highlight the specific gendered geography of *yatras* and the ways in which the leaders of the struggle outsourced women's issues to WMOs.

Chapter 5, on MASS, highlights the struggle of fishers against corporate capital and their success in gaining concessions from the company and the state, but not in preventing the construction of the power plant. MASS emerged before the protests against the power plant from the efforts of a community-based organization, Bhadreshwar SETU, with an explicit commitment to gender equality. Bhadreshwar SETU itself is a product of a regional network of NGOs. As a result of this nested local field of protest, MASS has ongoing relationships with several WMOs and NGOs, and as such has developed a productive strategy of ongoing engagement to address gender justice within and outside the struggle.

In the conclusion, I discuss the implications of the varied outcomes of the three struggles and their gendered geographies for democracy and development in India, as well as for scholarship on subaltern struggles against development, social movements, and gender.

Notes

1 We will give our lives but not our land!
2 The village land belongs to the village, not the government!
3 Save Our Water, Land, and Jungles
4 Literally, pilgrimage (yatra) by foot (pad) but is commonly used to refer to protest marches.
5 Subramanian (2009) first articulated this gender-neutral term to refer to both fisher women and men.
6 Neoliberal development, often referred to as liberalization in India, is characterized by privatization and the increasing role of the market and the declining role of the state in economic and social development. Yet, the state has retained an important role in selling common property resources, especially land, at highly subsidized rates to private corporations, becoming a "land broker state" (Levien 2014). I discuss in greater detail the particular character of neoliberalism in India and in Gujarat in Chapter 2.
7 The *Narmada Bachao Andolan* emerged in the mid-1980s to protest the construction of over 100 dams along the river Narmada and its tributaries. Its transnational mobilization resulted in the World Bank withdrawing its funding for the project in 1993. The Indian state, however, continued without World Bank funding, and most of the dams were completed in the 2000s. The movement still continues as the National Alliance of People's Movements to protest ongoing dispossession of subaltern groups in India (Baviskar 1995; Nilsen 2010).
8 This slogan itself has crossed over from the NBA and is heard in almost all contemporary movements against dispossession throughout India (Baviskar 1995; Levien 2013; Nilsen 2010).
9 This articulation has parallels to "new legal realism" in the US context (e.g., Merry 2006).
10 *Bhai* is the Gujarati word for brother and is usually used following the first name of a man as a polite and respectful form of address. *Dada* means paternal grandfather, and is a polite form of address for elderly men, while *ben*, meaning sister, is used as a polite form of address for women.

References

Alvarez, Sonia. 2009. "Beyond NGO-ization? Reflections from Latin America." *Development* 52:175–184.
Appadurai, Arjun. 1996. *Modernity at Large: Cultural Dimensions of Globalization.* Minneapolis: University of Minnesota Press.
Banarjee, Mukulika. 1999. "Democracy, an Indian Variant," available at http://les1.man.ac.uk/sa/Man99PolAnthPapers/Mukulika%2OBanerjee.htm.
Banaszak, Lee Ann, Karen Beckwith, and Dieter Rucht, editors. 2003. *Women's Movements Facing the Reconfigured State.* Cambridge: Cambridge University Press.
Basu, Amrita, editor. 2010. *Women's Movements in a Global Era: The Power of Local Feminisms.* Boulder: Westview Press.
———. 1992. *Two Faces of Protest: Contrasting Modes of Women's Activism in India.* New Delhi: University of California Press and Oxford University Press.
Baviskar, Amita. 1995. *In the Belly of the River: Tribal Conflicts over Development in the Narmada Valley.* Delhi: Oxford University Press.
Blecher, Michael. 2008. "Mind the Gap." *Law Critique* 19:297–306.
Chaterjee, Partha. 2010. "The State". *The Oxford Companion to Politics in India.* New Delhi: Oxford University Press.
———.1993. "Reflections on "Can the Subaltern Speak?": Subaltern Studies After Spivak." In *Can the Subaltern Speak: Reflections on the History of an Idea*, edited by Rosalind Morris, 81–86. New York: Columbia University Press.
Comaroff John L., and Jean Comaroff. 2009. "Reflections on the Anthropology of Law, Governance, and Sovereignty". In *Rules of Law and Laws of Ruling*, edited by Franz von Benda-Beckmann, Keebet von Benda-Beckmann and Julia Eckert, 31–60. Farnham: Ashgate.
Connell, Raewyn. 2011. *Confronting Equality: Gender, Knowledge and Global Change.* Cambridge: Polity Press.
Conway, Janet. 2013. *Edges of Global Justice: The World Social Forum and its Others.* London and New York: Routledge.
Corbridge, Stuart and John Harriss. 2000. *Reinventing India.* Cambridge: Polity Press.
Desai, Jigna, Danielle Bouchard, and Diane Detournay. 2010. "Disavowed Legacies and Honorable Thievery: The Work of the "Transnational" in Feminist and LGBT Studies." In *Critical Transnational Feminist Praxis*, edited by Amanda Lock Swarr and Richa Nagar, 46–64. Albany: State University of New York Press.
Desai, Manali. 2007. *State Formation and Radical Democracy in India.* London: Routledge.
Desai, Manisha. 2009. "From a Uniform Civil Code to Legal Pluralism: The Continuing Debates in India." In *Gender, Family, and Law in a Globalizing Middle East and South Asia*, edited by Ken Cuno and Manisha Desai. Syracuse: Syracuse University Press.
———. 2008 *Gender and the Politics of Possibilities: Rethinking Globalization.* Lanham: Rowman and Littlefield.

Eckert, Julia. 2006. "From Subjects to Citizens: Legalism From Below and the Homogenisation of the Legal Sphere." *Journal of Legal Pluralism* 53–54:45–75.

Eschle, Catherine and Bice Maiguashca. 2010. *Making Feminist Sense of the Global Justice Movement*. Langham: Rowman and Littlefield.

Escobar, Arturo. 2008. *Territories of Difference: Place, Movement, Life*, Redes. Durham: Duke University Press.

Esteva, Gustavo. 2007. "Oaxaca: The Path of Radical Democracy." *Socialism and Democracy* 21(2):74–96.

Evans, Sara. 1980. *Personal Politics: The Roots of Women's Liberation in the Civil Rights Movement and the New Left*. New York: Vintage.

Featherstone, David. 2008. *Resistance, Space and Political Identities: The Making of Counter-Global Networks*. Hoboken: Wiley-Blackwell.

Ferree, Myra Marx and Aili Mari Tripp, editors. 2006. *Global Feminism: Transnational Women's Activism, Organizing, and Human Rights*. New York: New York University Press. Princeton: Princeton University Press.

Frankel, Francine. 2005. *India's Political Economy*. Delhi: Oxford University Press.

Frankel, Francine and M. S. Rao. 1990. *Dominance and State Power in India: The Decline of a Social Order*. Delhi: Oxford University Press.

Gandhi, Nandita, and Nandita Shah. 1992. *The Issues at Stake: Theory and Practice in the Contemporary Women's Movement in India*. New Delhi: kali for Women.

Gillan, Kevin and Jenny Pickerill. 2012. "The Difficult and Hopeful Ethics of Research on, and with, Social Movements." *Social Movement Studies: Journal of Social, Cultural and Political Protest* 11:2, 133–143.

Guha, Ramachandra. 1989. *The Unquiet Woods*. Delhi: Oxford University Press.

Gupta, Akhil. 2012. *Red Tape: Bureaucracy, Structural Violence, and Poverty in India*. Durham: Duke University Press.

Heller, Patrick. 2005. "Reinventing Public Power in the Age of Globalization." In *Social Movements in India: Poverty, Power, and Politics*, edited by Raka Ray and Mary Fainsod Katzenstein, 79–106. Lanham: Rowman and Littlefield.

———. 1999. *Labor of Development*. Ithaca: Cornell University Press.

Horn, Jessica. 2013. *Gender and Social Movements: Overview Report*. Brighton: BRIDGE/Institute of Development Studies.

IFJP. 2005. *International Feminist Journal of Politics: Special Issue on Gender Mainstreaming* 7(4).

Jaffrelot, Christopher. 2003. *The Silent Revolution*. New York: Columbia University Press.

Jasper, James. 2013. "Introduction: Playing the Game." In *Players and Arenas: The Interactive Dynamics of Protest*, edited by Jan Willem Duyvendak and James Jasper, 4–29. Chicago: University of Chicago Press.

Jayawardena, Kumari. 1986. *Feminism and Nationalism in the Third World*. London: Zed Books.

Jessop, Bob. 2008. *State Power*. Cambridge: Polity Press.

Kaminski, Marek. 2004. *Games Prisoners Play*. Princeton: Princeton University Press.

Kardam, Nuket. 2004. "The Global Gender Equality Regime from Neoliberal and Constructivist Perspectives in International Relations." *International Feminist Journal of Politics* 6(1):85–109.

Kaviraj, Sudipta 1997. "A Critique of the Passive Revolution". In *State and Politics in India*, edited by Partha Chatterjee. New Delhi: Oxford University Press.
Kohli, Atul. 1987. *The State and Poverty in India*. Cambridge: Cambridge University Press.
Kothari, Rajni. 1989. *Politics and People: In Search of a Humane India, Vol.1*. New Delhi: Ajanta Publications.
———. 1984. "The Non-Party Political Process." *Economic and Political Weekly* 19(5):216–224.
Kumar, Radha. 1993. *History of Doing: An Illustrated Account of Movements for Women's Rights and Feminism in India, 1800–1990*. New Delhi: Kali for Women.
Kuumba, Bahati M. 2001. *Gender and Social Movements*. Walnut Creek: AltaMira Press.
Levien, Michael. 2014. "The Land Broker State: Dispossession and Development in Neoliberal India." Paper Presented at the American Sociological Association Annual Meeting, San Francisco, California, August 16–19.
———. 2013. "The Politics of Dispossession: Theorizing India's "Land Wars."" *Politics and Society* 41(3):351–394.
Maier, Elizabeth and Nathalie Lebon, editors. 2010. *Women's Activism in Latin American and the Caribbean: Engendering Social Justice, Democratizing Citizenship*. New Brunswick: Rutgers University Press. Tijuana: El Colegio De La Frontera Norte. A.C.
Martin, Isaac. 2013. *Rich People's Movements: Grassroots Campaigns to Untax the One Percent*. Oxford: Oxford University Press.
Mazumdar, Veena. 1985. *The Emergence of the Women's Question in India and the Role of Women's Studies*. Occasional Paper No. 7. New Delhi: Center for Women's Development Studies.
McBride, Dorothy and Amy Mazur. 2010. *The Politics of State Feminism: Innovation in Comparative Research*. Philadelphia: Temple University Press.
McFarlane, Colin. 2009. "Translocal Assemblages: Space, Power, and Social Movements." *Geoforum* 40(2009):561–567.
Menon, Nivedita. 2009. "Sexuality, Caste, Governmentality: Contests Over 'Gender' in India." *Feminist Review* 91:94–112.
———. 2004. *Recovering Subversion: Feminist Politics Beyond the Law*. Urbana: University of Illinois Press.
——— 1999. *Gender and Politics in India*. New Delhi: Oxford University Press.
Merry, Sally. 2006. "New Legal Realism and the Ethnography of Transnational law." *Law &Social Inquiry* 31(4):975–995.
Meszaros, George. 2013. *Social Movements, Law, and the Politics of Land Reform*. Cavendish: Routledge.
Moghadam, Valentine. 2012. *Globalization and Social Movements: Islamism, Feminism, and the Global Justice Movement*. Lanham: Rowman and Littlefield.
Mohanty, Chandra Talpade. 2003. *Feminism without Borders: Decolonizing Theory, Practicing Solidarity*. Durham: Duke University Press.
Mukherjee, Nirmalangshu. 2012. *The Maoist in India*. London: Pluto Press.
Mulqueen, Tara and Anastasia Tataryn. 2012. "Don't Occupy This Movement." *Law Critique* 23:283–298.

Nielsen, Kenneth. 2011. "Land, Law, Resistance," *Economic and Political Weekly* 46(41):38–40.

Nigam, Aditya and Nivedita Menon. 2007. *Power and Contestation: India since 1989*. London: Zed Books.

Nilsen Gunvald, Alf. 2012. "For a Historical Sociology of State-Society Relations in the Study of Subaltern Politics." Paper presented at the Workshop at the University of Connecticut.

———. 2010. *Dispossession and Resistance in India: The River and the Rage*. London: Routledge.

O'Brien, Kevin and Lianjiang Li. 2006. *Rightful Resistance in Rural China*. New York: Cambridge University Press.

Omvedt, Gail. 1993. *Reinventing Revolution: New Social Movements and the Socialist Tradition in India*. Armonk: M.E. Sharpe.

Paine, Thomas. 1992. *Rights of Man*. Indianapolis: Hackett.

Ray, Raka. 1999. *Fields of Protest: Women's Movements in India*. Minneapolis: University of Minnesota Press.

Ray, Raka and Mary Fainsod Katzenstein, editors. 2005. *Social Movements in India: Poverty, Power, and Politics*. Lanham: Rowman and Littlefield.

Robnett, Belinda. 2000. *How Long? How Long?: African-American Women in the Struggle for Civil Rights*. New York: Oxford University Press.

Sangari, Kum Kum and Sudesh Vaid, editors. 1989. *Recasting Women*. New Delhi: Kali for Women.

Santos, Boaventura de Sousa. 2014. "Southern Epistemologies: South-South, South-North, North-South Global Learnings." Presented at the International Colloquium on Epistemologies of the South, Coimbra, Portugal, 10–12 July.

———. 2002. *Toward a New Legal Common Sense: Law, Globalization, and Emancipation*. London: Butterworths.

Santos, Boaventura de Sousa and Cesar A. Rodriguez-Garavito, editors. 2005. *Law and Globalization from Below: Towards a Cosmopolitan Legality*. Cambridge: Cambridge University Press.

Sen, Ilina. 1990. *A Space Within the Struggle: Women's Participation in People's Movement*. New Delhi: Kali for Women.

Shah, Alpa. 2010. *In the Shadows of the State: Indigenous Politics, Environmentalism, and Insurgency in Jharkhand, India*. Durham and London: Duke University Press.

Sharma. Aradhana. 2008. *Logics of Empowerment: Development, Gender, and Governance in Neoliberal India*. Minneapolis: University of Minnesota Press.

Sharma, Shubra. 2011. *"Neoliberalism" As Betrayal: State, Feminism, and a Women's Educational Program in India*. London: Palgrave McMillan.

Sieder, Rachel and John Andrew McNeish, editors. 2012. *Gender Justice and Legal Pluralities: Latin American and African Perspectives*. London: Routledge.

Sinha, Mrinalini. 2012. "A Global Perspective on Gender: What's South Asia Got to Do with It?" In *South Asian Feminisms*, edited by Ania Loomba and Ritty Lukose, 356–374. Durham and London: Duke University Press.

Snyder, Margaret. 2006. *Unlikely Godmother: The UN and the Global Women's Movement*. In *Global Feminism: Transnational Women's Activism, Organizing, and Human Rights*, edited by Myra Marx Ferree and Aili Mari Tripp, 24–50. New York: New York University Press.

Spivak, Gayatri. 2012. *An Aesthetic Education in the Era of Globalization.* Cambridge: Harvard University Press.

Subramanian, Ajantha. 2009. *Shorelines: Space and Rights in South India.* Stanford: Stanford University Press.

Taylor, Verta. 1999. "Gender and Social Movements: Gender Processes in Women's Self-Help Movements." *Gender & Society* 13(1): 8–33.

Tilly, Charles. 2008. *Contentious Performances.* Cambridge: Cambridge University Press.

Tripp, Aili Mari, Isabel Casimiro, Joy Kwesiga, and Alice Mungwa, editors. 2009. *African Women's Movements: Changing Political Landscapes.* Cambridge: Cambridge University Press

Walby, Sylvia. 2013. *The Future of Feminism.* Cambridge: Polity Press.

———. 2005. "Introduction: Comparative Gender Mainstreaming in a Global Era." *International Feminist Journal of Politics* 7(4):453–470.

Whittier, Nancy. 2007. "Gender and Social Movements." *The Blackwell Encyclopedia of Sociology*, 1872–1875.

Witsoe, Jeffrey. 2013. *Democracy against Development: Lower-Caste Politics and Political Modernity in Postcolonial India.* Chicago: University of Chicago Press.

Yadav, Yogendra. 2000. "The Second Democratic Surge," In *Transforming India*, edited by Francine Frankel, Zoya Hasan, Rajeev Bhargava, and Balveer Arora. New Delhi: Oxford University Press.

Yulia, Zemlinskaya. 2010. "Social Movements through the Gender Lens." *Sociology Compass* 4(18):628–641.

2 The making of translocal fields of protest

Quoting the opposition leader from Congress in Gujarat, Shakti Singh Gohil, Mehta (2011) notes:

> Gujaratis are a people of movements. From the Mahagujarat movement of the 1950s that demanded a separate linguistic state of Gujarat, the anti-corruption Navnirman movement of the 1970s, the anti-reservation agitations of the 1980s to the Ramjanmabhoomi campaign of the 1990s, Gujarat has been a hotbed of mass movements.
>
> (Mehta, 2011: 53)

With the exception of the early phase of the *Nav Nirman* (reconstruction) movement, however, the rest of the mass mobilizations sought to reinforce Hindu upper-caste and middle-class hierarchies and have contributed to what Mehta (2011) calls a coercive nativism. But alongside these mass mobilizations there have been other mobilizations, in particular, the Narmada Bacho Andolan, women's, environmental, and Gandhian movements, that have challenged the status quo.

Both sets of mass mobilizations were a product of the contradictions of India's changing development policies and democratic practices, which sought to address the conditions of the poor and marginalized subaltern communities but were driven by elite and middle-class considerations (e.g., Frankel, 2005; Kohli, 2009). And each set of mobilizations left behind social imaginaries, social movement organizations, non-governmental organizations (NGOs), advocates, and supporters that constitute the translocal fields of protest in both India and Gujarat.

From Nehruvian socialism to neoliberalism: the changing nature of the Indian state

Following independence from British colonial rule in 1947, India embarked on a Nehruvian instead of Gandhian[1] model of "modern" development that focused on mixed private and state-led industrialization by import substitution policies, and where the state also had a central role in addressing issues of poverty and inequity defined by caste, gender, and religion. Five Year Plans at the national level were formulated to outline the state's responsibilities. A mixed economy ensured space for the private sector alongside the public sector, but also regulated it, leading to the era of "license raj," which some critics argue resulted in the sluggish "Hindu rate of growth" (Kohli, 2009).

This model was elaborated and implemented primarily by upper-caste Hindu actors and excluded the vast majority of people, leading to what Motta and Nilsen (2011), borrowing from Gramsci, call an "unstable equilibrium" between the state and the elite. Along with this economic policy, the Nehruvian model included a secular, democratic polity that addressed through constitutional mechanisms the long-standing subaltern issues of social injustices of caste, gender, and religion. Reservations in education and government employment, along with credit for business, were established to enable members of "Scheduled Castes" and "Scheduled Tribes," so-called because of the lists (or "schedules") that enumerated the groups that were protected, to become full citizens of a new nation.

Yet, for many subaltern groups this was a subservient inclusion in the nation. From 1945–1951 the Telangana movement of peasants and *adivasis* in the state of Andhra Pradesh was the first to challenge the new nation. It redistributed land, refused to pay debts, and prevented forest officials from entering their areas. In response, the Indian army, constitutionally formed only in 1950, marched into Telangana to quell the struggle in 1951. D'Souza (2011) argues that this action demonstrates that the nation and its social contract, despite its socialist rhetoric, were based on the exclusion of the subaltern from the very beginning.

Kohli (2009), by contrast, argues that from the 1950s to 1960s the contradiction between socialist rhetoric and capitalist practices favoring the elites strengthened democracy as the powerful felt served and the poor did not yet feel excluded. He argues that the national civil service and the Congress party both contributed to a stable government and established democratic roots in the nation. Although the Congress's base was the landed elites, the lower caste and poor majority who depended on them for their livelihoods seldom opposed them, with Telangana and Tebhaga being exceptions. Ray and Katzenstein (2005) also argue that from 1947–1964, when Nehru oversaw the functioning of the new nation, most social movements worked through the Congress party and with the state. They argue that during this phase, social movements such as the labor movement, cooperative movement, and women's movements that focused on poverty worked by accommodating the state's redistributive frame, even as it meant supporting the interests of the elite against those of the poor.

Despite some early success through infrastructure and manufacturing investments, the economy continued to stall and poverty remained and continues to be a major issue (e.g., Kohli, 2009; Menon and Nigam, 2007). The failure of this model to address issues of poverty and growth led to its unraveling by the 1960s. Scholars have attributed this failure to, among other factors, a gendered division of labor that devalued and erased women's paid and unpaid labor in the home and outside, as well as excluding the urban informal sector and the rural poor (e.g., Menon and Nigam, 2007; Motta and Nilsen, 2011). As a result, new movements emerged in India to challenge the persistent poverty and exclusion of the subaltern classes.

The 1967 Naxalbari peasant uprising, influenced by Maoism in West Bengal, was the first such movement to argue that the social contract could not work for the peasants, *adivasis*, and the urban poor. Moreover, they argued that liberal parliamentary democracy not only could not meet the aspirations of the most marginalized, but also that it was as tyrannical for them as the colonial government that it replaced. India's elite and ruling classes, they argued, would not abdicate power, and only a revolution could forge a new India (D'Souza, 2011).

Whereas the Naxalbari movement engaged in revolutionary violence, including killing landlords, Jai Prakash Narayan's "total revolution"[2] was based on Gandhian principles of non-violence and *gram swaraj* (village self-rule). He saw power flowing from below to make the state accountable. This period saw the emergence of movements around a variety of issues and identities across the country. For example, SEWA (the Self Employed Women's Association) in Ahmedabad organized informal sector women, the *Chipko* movement sought to protect forests and livelihoods from timber merchants, the *Chhatra Yuva Sangharsh Vahini* (Vehicle for Youth Struggle) in Bihar sought land for the landless, the *Nav Nirman* student movement in Gujarat fought against corruption and rise in food prices, and *Dalit* (literally oppressed, those outside the caste system) Panthers in Maharashtra challenged caste-based injustices (e.g., Omvedt 1993, Ray and Katzenstein 2005).

What these and other movements of the late 1960s and early 1970s shared were discourses and practices about "reinventing participatory democracy as social action and political practice and creating new spaces and infusing deeper meaning into democracy" (Sheth, 2007: 3). They sought to democratize development and democracy through Non-Party Political Formations and were often led by educated urban middle classes who organized on behalf of and with the poor. As Omvedt (1993) noted, they were reinventing revolution, informed by Marxist ideas but extending them to include caste, gender, environmental sustainability, and other identities and issues excluded by parties of the left. These movements were in active communication with each other through alternative media such as newsletters, journals, and collective dialogues, leading to the formation of several translocal fields of protest.

In response to such protests as well as the dissension within the Congress party, Indira Gandhi consolidated power by splitting the Congress party and making it a tool for her own power. She also adopted a populist rhetoric of *Garibi Hatao* (abolish poverty), and nationalized banks, and abolished the princely privy purses. When these measures did not quell the protests in the country, she ultimately declared a national emergency in 1975, arrested opposition leaders and activists, and launched a forced sterilization program to address population increase, which was seen as a factor in the continuing poverty. When elections were held in 1977 the *Janata* (People's) Party – a coalition of parties that ranged from the socialist to the Hindu nationalist Jana Sangh, a precursor to the Bharatiya Janata Party (BJP) – defeated the Congress party at the national level. But internal conflicts within the coalition led to its fragmentation and the return of the Congress party to power in 1980. But it was at the state level that the lower caste and *dalit* parties began to dominate politics. Gujarat, however, did not see the emergence of such regional parties. As Sanghavi (2011) notes, it has always been a bipolar state moving between the two national parties, Congress and BJP. And in response to strong centralization by Indira Gandhi, there were also many subnational movements for autonomy and secession.

Following her reelection after the Emergency, in 1980 Indira Gandhi not only continued to consolidate political power, but also changed her populist rhetoric and aligned more openly with the capitalist class. Kohli (2009) argues that it was this state–capitalist alliance, energized by Indira Gandhi and then supported by Rajiv Gandhi after her assassination in 1984, that initiated economic growth beginning in 1980, and not the neoliberal policies adopted in 1991. He argues that from being a reluctant pro-capitalist state with socialist ideology under Nehru, India became a pro-capitalist state under Indira Gandhi, and then finally adopted a neoliberal ideology and opened its economy to foreign capital under Narasimha Rao in 1991. Even when the Congress party was replaced by the Hindu nationalist BJP at the national level in 1998, the economic priorities did not change. What changed was the rhetoric of all parties: from democratic socialism to pro-business market orientation.

Unlike other developing countries, however, in India the shift from a development state to a neoliberal state has not been linear or unidirectional. Although it has included reducing tariffs, liberalizing foreign investment laws, and cutting some public expenditures – for example, food subsidies – under the rhetoric of inclusive development, the state has also increased public expenditures through employment guarantee schemes and poverty alleviation programs for people living below the poverty line (e.g., Gupta and Sivaramakrishnan, 2010; Sharma, 2008).

> In the standard narrative of neoliberalism, the emphasis has always been on the slashing of public expenditures by cost-conscious governments, not on increasing public outlays for people to meet basic needs. One could argue that this is a peculiar outcome of Indian democracy because voter participation for poor, subaltern, and rural groups is higher than for urban, middle class people, and numerically poor and rural groups form a preponderant part of the electorate.
> (Gupta and Sivaramakrishnan, 2010: 5)

At the same time, with the increasing fragmentation of the polity, represented by the declining power of Congress and the increasing power of regional parties, the ruling alliance has become a narrow group of technocrats and big business (Kohli, 2009). India's highest and most competent bureaucratic elite thus works on behalf of the elite and middle classes, whereas the state and local-level bureaucrats work for their own personal and community interests. As a result, despite an increase in programs for the poor, they experience the state not only as ineffective and corrupt, but also as coercive (Kohli, 2009). And when it does work on their behalf, the poor are seen as beneficiaries of state development rather than as citizens with rights. This "development altruism" (Menon, 2009) is so pervasive that even when the subaltern groups win elections they are seen as development managers rather than political leaders.

For the subaltern groups, then, the changes in the Indian state from socialism to neoliberalism have meant access to some resources but also loss of lands and livelihoods, with uneven compensation in the process of development by dispossession. But such practices of the state have not gone unchallenged. Peasants, *adivasis*, and farmers all across the country have used a variety of strategies to resist such displacement, fight for their rights as citizens, and articulate an alternative development that is more inclusive. Thus, despite the importance of the market and religious nationalism that holds sway in India today, the subaltern struggles represent a challenge to it.

But as my research shows and Heller (2005) argues, new subaltern movements are not anti-development, as post-colonial critics claim, but rather they "remain centrally concerned with expanding the role of public powers to underwrite social citizenship" (Heller, 2005: 80). Like older movements of the late 1960s and 1970s, they are committed to a political project of expanding social citizenship and engaging with the state, but doing so on terms that include them in administrative, political, and financial decision making, hence deepening democratic participation. Decentralizing state functions, what Heller (2005) calls redistribution from below, has not replaced redistribution from above. Although decentralization has also been a tool deployed by neoliberal economic reforms, social movements' ability to claim it and link it with a vision of democratic empowerment and expansion of public decision making is an important contribution to this effort.

In a similar vein, Sheth (2007) argues that the contemporary subaltern struggles, are also about repoliticizing development and reinventing participatory democracy:

> [T]hey now view development as a political struggle for the people's participation in defining development goals and devising means to achieve them. Their view of development is thus a non-hegemonic, pluralistic process, in articulating which they use insights inductively arrived at and criteria that have evolved through their own struggles.
>
> (Sheth, 2007: 15)

These movements also debate feminism, ecology, and human rights but are no longer influenced by pre-modern nostalgia and old post-colonial critique, and build translocal alliances that seek to link rural poverty to patterns of urban growth. These movements have been facilitated by the changing legal architecture that has enabled them to engage in legalism from below.

The legal architecture of deepening democracy

By legal architecture, I refer specifically to the *panchayati raj* legislation, the activism of the Supreme Court, and the mobilization that resulted in the Right to Information Act. Beginning in the post-Emergency era, these changes influenced in part by the subaltern politics of the late 1960s and 1970s have provided opportunities for legalism from below, which contemporary subaltern struggles have utilized with a fair degree of success. I address each of these changes in the following sections.

Panchayati raj legislation

From the founding of the nation, leaders were interested in local governance, or *panchayati raj*.[3] Mahatma Gandhi in particular distrusted central authority in a country as large and rural as India. At his behest, *panchayats* were inserted into the constitution in Article 40, and the Balwant Mehta Committee was appointed to study their viability via community development programs (Visvanathan and Parmar, 2005). Even Nehru expressed interest in decentralization and incorporated it into the National Planning Commission (Kothari, 1989). By 1959 all states had a Panchayat Act, and by the mid-1960s more than 217,300 villages covering 92% of India had formal *panchayat* systems (Manor, 2010). But in reality, given the immense poverty, lack of formal education, and the vastness of the country, most *panchayats* were ineffective and corrupt. Within the next decade they were in decline, as there was no institutional effort to fund them or to hold regular elections.

Decentralization efforts were revived at the national and state levels following the experience of national Emergency. The 1977 elections saw the defeat of the Congress party at both the national and state levels. At the national level, the newly elected Janata Party, the first non-Congress party to rule the Centre since independence, expressed interest in decentralization legislation, but due to internal conflicts did not manage to act on it. But in 1977 the Communist Party of India (Marxist) in West Bengal and in 1983 the Janata Party in Karnataka enacted *panchayati raj* legislations in their states (Manor, 2010). Following the return to power of the Congress party, Rajiv Gandhi's government also expressed some interest in decentralization in 1985, but it was not until the election year of 1989 that he focused on it. He was assassinated while campaigning for that election and the V. P. Singh government that followed introduced a single bill towards that end but was not able to see it through, as the government fell due to controversies over reservation.

It was the Congress government under Narasimha Rao that in 1991 submitted the same two bills drafted earlier to pay homage to Rajiv Gandhi. With support from all parties, the 73rd and 74th amendments to the constitution, in support of democratic decentralization for rural and urban sectors, respectively, were passed and came into force in 1993. Since local government is a state subject under the constitution, it was up to each state government to respond to the amendments. In Gujarat, Modi in particular has tried to bring a market sensibility to the process by promoting *samras*, or no-election, *panchayats* based on consensus among the local community. Different states have devolved power and resources to different extents. This undermines the spirit of the legislation but nonetheless provides space for an active citizenry. Today, there are 2 million elected representatives in various local governments (Manor, 2010). Along with the reservation for Scheduled Castes and Tribes, this decentralization has indeed provided space for subaltern groups to participate in local governance.

Thus, the history of democratic decentralization in India predates the global rhetoric of decentralization and good governance emanating from the neoliberal regimes in the West (Manor, 2010). Rather, it represents a much more local and complex political history. Studies that have assessed the implementation and success of this experiment note the importance of resources and actual power and accountability mechanisms in how successful it can be for ordinary people, particularly subaltern groups.

The ripple effects of the Panchayati Raj bills could be seen on various other laws. In April 1997 the government passed the Environment Public Hearing (EPH) amendment to the 1986 Environment Protection Law, enacted following the World Summit on Environment held in 1972 in Stockholm (Pandey, 2003). This amendment requires thirty types of industries, especially infrastructure, chemicals, and other polluting industries, to hold an Environment Public Hearing before it can get environmental clearance from the National Ministry of Environment and Forests. Such hearings were meant to promote democratic participation in keeping with the Panchayati Raj Act. Before the EPH, the act required that an Environmental Impact Assessment (EIA) be conducted and an Environmental Management Plan (EMP) be formulated. But until 1997, the EIA and EMP were to be filed only with the ministry. Following the amendment, they are now to be available more widely to the people living in the affected area.

This amendment also outlined in detail the process for such hearings and how to ensure that all stakeholders had access to this information. Given the bureaucratic and expert knowledge involved, NGOs play an important role as advocates to inform the public, prepare plans and analyses, and anticipate conflict resolution means. NGOs identify Project Affected People (PAP) and then work with them to conduct baseline studies, evaluate the impact of a given project, prepare a mitigation plan, compare alternatives, and come to a decision about the proposed project. Such public hearings have become key sites of protest for subaltern groups throughout the country, as well as the struggles in this book.

Yet, a study of twenty public hearings undertaken by the Center for Social Justice in Gujarat (Pandey, 2003) found that it was difficult to get access to the summaries and have adequate time to prepare for public hearings. Hence, under public interest litigation the center filed a case to highlight the problems with the EPH. In particular, they highlighted that information about the time and place of the hearing was not circulated widely or with adequate time to enable the affected people to prepare a response. The *Center for Social Justice v. Union of India* 1999 case led to a landmark judgment in 2000 which directed the state government and the Pollution Board of Gujarat to mandate transparency in a venue of public hearing by publishing the announcement in the local language in at least two newspapers thirty days prior to the hearing and ensuring the recording and dissemination of the minutes in the local language. Advocacy groups like the Center for Social Justice continue to work on addressing loopholes in the process.

34 *Making translocal fields of protest*

These decentralization efforts have been facilitated, albeit in contradictory ways, by the activism of the Supreme Court of India.

Supreme Court activism

In addition to democratic decentralization, the Supreme Court (SC) of India has been a major actor in expanding subaltern democratic participation. Defined by one scholar as "chemotherapy for the carcinogenic body politic" (Baxi, 2003, cited in Rajamani and Sengupta, 2010: 80), Rajamani and Sengupta (2010) argue that from a modest institution at independence the SC has become a "powerful, dynamic actor that shapes law, evolves policy, and plays a central determinative role in the governance of modern India" (p. 80). They date the beginning of Supreme Court activism to the late 1970s following the end of the Emergency. Before then, to consolidate her rule, Indira Gandhi enacted laws that established parliamentary (essentially her) supremacy over the SC. The SC for the most part went along with her efforts and against the opposition, in the process losing any legitimacy as an independent institution. Following the end of the Emergency in 1977, the SC sought popular legitimacy rather than constitutional legitimacy to gain back its reputation.

One of the chief ways it did so was through Public Interest Litigation (PIL), which was meant to enable ordinary people access to the nation's highest judicial body. PIL essentially changed the requirement of *locus standi*, from those aggrieved to those defending citizens and the poor and holding the government accountable.

> Public interest litigation has come to be characterized by a collaborative approach, procedural flexibility, judicially-supervised interim orders, and forward looking relief. . . And, they typically involve numerous parties and stakeholders, amicus curiae, and fact-finding/expert/monitoring/policy-evolution committees.
> (Rajamani and Sengupta, 2010: 86)

Given its power and resources the SC can set in motion investigative and policy evolution processes and can continue to monitor an issue via committees.

But for PIL to be effective, substantive rights have to be comprehensive, and so the SC has expanded these rights over the last three decades. In particular, the SC has expanded Article 21, the right to life and liberty, to mean life with human dignity that includes rights to livelihood, education, health, and pollution-free water and air. It has also widened remedies for violations from merely making declarations to legislative remedies under Article 32,

Making translocal fields of protest 35

enforcement of fundamental rights. It has also functioned as an executive. Unlike Indira Gandhi who challenged an activist Supreme Court, under the current political climate of coalition rule with no party holding a majority and the SC's popular legitimacy derived from expanding rights, no party has challenged the SC. This may change with the recent victory of BJP with an unprecedented majority.

Yet, Rajamani and Sengupta (2010) argue that such judicial activism by the Supreme Court has serious flaws, particularly in relation to its rulings around environmental protections. For example, they argue that although the SC is seen to have "fostered an extensive and innovative jurisprudence on environmental rights," justices have not articulated a coherent philosophy of environmental law. Moreover, they have not provided any guidelines on how to balance the need for development with the need for protection and conservation of natural resources. Rather, justices have molded and expanded the right to fit the case rather than lay down boundaries. Such a case-by-case approach, they argue, has led to imprecision and intellectual fuzziness that does not offer guidance on value-laden judgments about ecocentric versus anthropocentric values. This, they note, has resulted in a strong call to action without enforceable legal obligation. "Increased discretionary space, imprecise rights, unclear obligations, and fuzzy principles lend themselves to judgments based on predilections rather than principle" (Rajamani and Sengupta, 2010: 90).

Moreover, critics argue that given the SC's middle-class bias, it is more receptive to certain issues than others such as clean environment rather than livelihood and technical modes of argumentation rather than social claims.

> This is indeed ironic given the origins of judicial activism and PIL in India. The Court opened its doors and liberalized locus standi in the late 1970s to address the 'problem of the poor.' Yet, today, several decades on, it is the problems of the middle class that are most likely to be viewed sympathetically by the Courts.
> (Rajamani and Sengupta, 2010: 91)

As my analysis shows, however, this is not entirely the case. The SC has ruled in favor of subaltern groups on the basis of livelihood.

But given its new activism, the SC relies on socio-legal and expert committees for fact gathering, expert advice, and monitoring along with policy evolution. These ad hoc committees include judges, lawyers, health professionals, and bureaucrats and often lead to inconsistencies and inequities, and few offer public participation. This claim is also belied by the struggles in this study. Critics of SC activism are especially troubled by its overreach. They claim that it has taken on legislative issues it is ill equipped to handle and in fact is undemocratic. Mehta (2007) calls this formal judicial supremacy and sees it as a cause for concern. He argues that such supremacy does not lead to a constitutional culture that imposes principled limits on government or individuals. PIL cases involve many affected parties and not all can be brought before the courts and hence the courts need to demonstrate restraint. Critics also argue that such cases do little to underscore the lack of routine access to justice for most people.

Although this is undeniable, social movements have been inspired by the SC activism to engage in legalism from below and seek legislative redress for some of their issues, as was the case with the Right to Information (RTI) Act.

Right to Information Act

The Right to Information Act is an important instance of legalism from below resulting in new legislation. First initiated by *Mazdoor Kisan Shakti Sangathan* (Worker and Farmers Empowerment Organization, henceforth MKSS) in Rajasthan to address issues of local corruption, it soon became a national movement culminating in the passage of the Right to Information Act in 2005 in the Indian parliament. MKSS formed in 1990 to use struggle and constructive action to change the lives of the rural poor. Towards this goal, they had initiated two hunger strikes for just pay for work on public works programs.

> But it was also in this fight for the payment of the statutory minimum wage under government-sponsored public works programmes that the group first understood the significance of transparency and the right to information. Every time the workers asked to be paid the minimum wage, they were told that they had not done the work, a claim that, they were also told, was based on records. When the MKSS demanded to see the records, the reply was that these were government accounts and therefore secret.
>
> (Roy and Dey, 1999: 4)

Government documents were protected by the colonial-era Official Secrets Act of 1923.

So it was in the struggle for wages that the right to information emerged. MKSS then mobilized a *dharna* (sit-in) for fifty-three days in 1996, an election year, to demand an amendment in the Panchayati Raj Act to allow citizens a photocopy of any document in local government offices, especially expenditures like bills, vouchers, and muster rolls. Chanting "the right to know, the right to live," those on strike were able to understand the importance of information not only to their livelihood but also to their ability to be active citizens in a democracy. The strike resulted in success as the state government passed the right to information, albeit with numerous loopholes. This did not prevent the citizens from proudly carrying a copy of the *Gazette*, which announced the new law. "In concrete terms, at a local level, it has helped demonstrate the conceptual difference between decentralization and self-government" (Roy and Dey, 2008: 210).

MKSS did not stop with the passage of the law. Rather, it held a public hearing, a *jan sunwai*, to discuss the documents they were able to get from the local office. During the meeting, activists read and analyzed the documents together with the villagers. Organized independently of the mandatory *gram sabha*, village council meetings, they invited local politicians and officials. Villagers also testified to highlight the discrepancy between government records and their realities. As Roy and Dey (1999) describe it, in that first *jan sunwai*, the mood changed from puzzlement to anger. Seeing the fury of the people, even before the meeting ended, a woman *sarpanch*, elected chief of the local body, returned Rs. 100,000. What the fear of the law or arrest could not stop, the fear of people did. Such *jan sunwais*, platforms of collective discussions, have become a critical part of the repertoire of movements across the state and the country.

Following this success, MKSS initiated the National Campaign for People's Right to Information. In 1997, two draft Freedom of Information bills were introduced at the national level. This was not the first time that such a bill was debated in India. It was first discussed during the first non-Congress government between 1977 and 1979, and then by the V. P. Singh government in 1989–1990 and again from 1996–1998 by the United Front Coalition government.

As Jenkins and Goetz (1999) observe, before the MKSS struggle, the right to information was conceived in terms of free speech like in liberal democracies of the West and in keeping with Article 19 of the International Covenant on Civil and Political Rights, which links freedom of expression to seek, receive, and impart information and ideas of all kinds. Hence, the earlier bills were more about censorship rather than transparency. MKSS put the right to information in the context of right to life and livelihood. Their efforts to show that the right to information can be used by ordinary people and that it can be done so collectively changed its importance in struggles throughout the country, as evident in the protests in this book.

> The right to information movement in Rajasthan has offered hope to people striving to generate the culture, institutions and principles necessary for a participatory democracy. The RTI is finally a demand for an equal share of power. But it is also a fetter on the arbitrary exercise

of power by anyone. Its legitimacy in a democratic set-up gives it the potential to keep widening the horizons of struggles for empowerment and change. This legitimacy is strengthened further by its capacity to make transparent and accountable the user of the right as much as the power centre being held accountable.

(Roy and Dey, 1999: 17)

In a review of the RTI four years after its passage, Roberts (2010) notes that Indians filed 2 million requests and despite lack of public awareness, poor public planning and bureaucratic indifference and hostility, people and NGOs have developed useful innovations to access information. Two national and six regional studies, conducted between 2007 and 2009, show that citizens and civil organizations have been able to use the RTI to fight mismanagement and corruption and improve government responsiveness (Roberts 2010).

In Gujarat, there was indifference and hostility from the bureaucrats, who see it as a nuisance at best and at worst as challenging entrenched power relations. Most bureaucrats resist training, and 80% of those surveyed did not know of its proactive disclosure component and railed against it by saying: "Even God does not give anything unless someone asks him" (Roberts, 2010: 930). Most local officials charged fees for what was to be freely available and even after that did not follow through. As a result, some states are putting in place innovative practices such as automated cell phone updates on a request, as is the case in Andhra Pradesh, and opening *jaankari*, or information centers. RTI also applies to non-state actors performing state functions and is incorporated into other laws. As Sarangi (2012) notes, RTI is not just a quiet revolution in governance but a loud revolution in accountability, citizenship, and livelihood as evident in the three struggles in Gujarat.

The terrain of protest in Gujarat

Although Gujarat, the home of Mahatma Gandhi and his non-violent struggle for national liberation, is often seen as having a pacifist culture, the very formation of the post-independent state of Gujarat in 1960,[4] a result of popular mobilization, involved violence and the death of twenty-eight people (Yagnik and Sheth, 2005). Moreover, as Sanghavi (2011:15) notes, in Saurashtra, where two thirds of Gujarat's population lived, people experienced the "worst examples of petty tyranny and obscurantism and were never covered under the Gandhian image." Such violence has continued to mark Gujarati politics with the massacre of 1,100 Muslims in 1969, which, until the 2002 genocide of over 1,000 Muslims, was the worst such atrocity.

The student-led *Nav Nirman* movement similarly ended in violence in 1974 with the death of 103 people. Between 1974 and 1984, there were anti-government, anti-*dalit*, anti-reservation, and anti-Muslim riots with their attendant violence. Since 1995, the BJP has held power with its own form of violence, which Mehta (2011) calls "coercive nativism" against all others, especially the Muslims.

Despite this history of violent politics, the new state, composed of three administrative units of Gujarat, Saurashtra (also known as Kathiawad), and Kutch, became the center of the national model of modern development articulated by Nehru (Sud, 2010). But even before independence, from about 1857, Gujarat along with West Bengal and Tamil Nadu were industrially the most advanced. After independence, it undertook rapid expansion of heavy industries, infrastructure (particularly roads and dams), and modernization of agriculture through "green revolution." Gujarat and two adjoining states were the site of the Narmada Valley Dams Project, which Nehru called "temples of development." Additionally, the state subsidized the production of cash crops like groundnuts, cotton, and sugarcane, and began to implement land reform and redistribution under the slogan of "land to the tiller." Despite resistance from the landed elite, in Saurashtra and Kutch 1.2 million hectares of land were transferred from princes and large landowners to tenant farmers (Sud, 2010).

Gujarat's leaders adopted two strategies that enabled the state to register healthy growth rates even during the period of state regulation (Sinha, 2005). First, through bureaucratic innovations, such as the License Monitoring Cell created in 1969, they garnered a larger share of national monies. They were among the first states to have a national presence of high-level bureaucrats who, through infiltration of the central bureaucracy, informal communication channels, and flexible alternatives courted investors and national bureaucrats. Other innovations such as the Export Corporation and Non-Resident Indian investment cells created in 1965 and the industrial extension bureau, which engaged in industrial intelligence in competition with Maharashtra, also enabled it to become an industrial leader from the early days of its founding in 1960.

Second, from the beginning the state encouraged joint partnerships with the private sector, resulting in a mutually supportive relationship between the two. Hence, the private sector did not see the state merely as a constraint and was incorporated into the state. This also encouraged the public-sector firms to perform efficiently, which they did. As a result, when the national monies began to decline, it did not affect Gujarat as much. Sinha (2005) argues that Gujarat adopted this market-based and state-led strategy as early as 1968–1969. In addition to the usual incentives such as tax breaks, subsidies, and credit, it developed land, local markets, and training centers for industries. All these are in keeping with its mercantile culture. As Sinha (2005: 116) notes, "In Gujarat a bureaucrat behaves as if he is a businessman, while in West Bengal a businessman acts like a bureaucrat."

In Gujarat, as elsewhere, the beneficiaries of this rapid development were the upper castes, particularly the *Patidar-Kanbi* castes, which dominated politics and the economy. This state-led development prioritized industrialization and new institutions to support it, but did not address issues of the environment or equity and, although dispersed, the industrialization was concentrated in central and south Gujarat. Many lower classes and castes were able to make some gains through the small-scale ventures and, as a result, poverty and unemployment remained low. The labor movement remained Gandhian in orientation and hence was more accommodating than confrontational. Relatively successful land reforms meant that there was a large group of small farmers, 72% own fewer than thirty acres, and even *adivasis* were able to make some gains through government service and small-scale contracting.

But the rapid industrialization was accompanied by rapid urbanization and migration, which reproduced caste- and religion-based residential communities in the cities. Simultaneously, heavy industrialization, particularly in petroleum refining and chemicals, supported by medium-scale industrialization based on state subsidies meant that by the 1980s Gujarat was one of the most industrialized states in the country and aspired to become a "mini Japan" (Yagnik and Sheth, 2005). As the cities grew, so did corruption. Food prices rose and violent demonstrations broke out several times in the 1960s in Ahmedabad, Gujarat's largest city. These demonstrations, based on urban economic and social issues, became communalized. Between 1960 and 1969, there were 2,938 instances of communal violence, most in 1969 in which 1,100 Muslims were massacred (Sanghavi, 2011).

> The riots of 1969 took Gujarati society past the psychological threshold of normally tolerable public violence and this not only of communal variety... Once the barrier [of violence] was crossed, its repeated use acquired a tacit legitimacy as the Social Conscience became gradually more immune to the incremental dose of it.
> (Hemant Babu, 2003; cited in Sanghavi, 2011: 15)

These mass killings were followed in 1974 by the *Nav Nirman* student movement. But unlike the previous violence, which was based on communal identities, here Hindus and Muslims united to lead a movement against rising prices and corruption in the government. Among the leaders of this movement were Manishi Jani and Achyut Yagnik, key actors of the left in Gujarat today and who are both engaged in the three struggles analyzed in this book.

In addition to street protests and hunger strikes, the staple of protests, this movement used innovative tactics such as mock trials of corrupt officers and merchants who hoarded food while people were going hungry. They also led a parade of sheep and donkeys to symbolize politicians who meekly followed leaders. Students dressed as surgeons performed mock brain surgery to release grains and oil hoarded by merchants and money hoarded by the chief minister. They borrowed from the repertoire of the nationalist struggle, using *prabhat pheris*, morning rallies, to herald a new dawn of clean politics, and women banged pots and pans to call an end to the corruption by leaders and merchants. This student-led movement was soon infiltrated by underground criminal elements and political leaders and ended in violence as quickly as it had emerged, after only seventy-three days (Sanghavi, 2011). Although short lived, it caught the attention of well-known Gandhian leader Jay Prakash Narayan who, inspired by it, launched his total revolution movement in Bihar, which then spread across North India.

In response to their demands, the primarily upper-caste, ruling Congress party began to form a coalition of lower castes and Muslims, called, by its acronym, KHAM, *Kshatriyas* (primarily, lower warrior castes), *Harijans*,[5] and Muslims (Mehta and Mehta, 2011; Sanghavi, 2011; Simpson and Kapadia, 2010; Yagnik and Sheth, 2005). This resulted in the election of the state's first Congress chief minister from the lower caste. The changing composition of the Congress party alienated the upper castes, who shifted their allegiance to the BJP.

Along with this new coalition came a renewed focus on "reservation," a national program of affirmative action for the lower castes and *adivasis* (non-caste tribes). Whereas nationally the focus on reservation came from regional lower-caste parties, in Gujarat it was the Congress party that was responsible for enacting reservations. As a result, by 1985, in Gujarat 49% of seats in government professional colleges were reserved for the Scheduled Castes and Tribes. This led to violent protests by upper-caste but economically marginal students, citing reverse discrimination. The BJP capitalized on this and turned a class-based conflict into a communal one, channeling their opposition to the Congress into opposition of groups supported by Congress, primarily the Muslims (Yagnik and Sheth, 2005). In the 1980s as the BJP gained momentum nationally, Gujarat became its epicenter, resulting in large mobilizations and rallies against Muslims, many of which resulted in violence.

It was also during the 1980s that two new movements emerged in Gujarat that have cast a long shadow on Gujarati politics and contributed to its translocal field of protest. They were the pro-dam Narmada movement and the anti-dam *Narmada Bachoa Andolan* (NBA). The Narmada Valley Dams Project was proposed in 1959 as a solution to Western India's water crisis.

42 *Making translocal fields of protest*

Consisting of 30 major, 135 medium, and 3,000 small dams on the river Narmada and its tributaries, the foundation stone of this mega-project was laid by Nehru in 1961 (Baviskar, 1995). But the actual construction of the dams did not begin until 1980 due to, among other reasons, disputes about water distribution among the three states through which the river flows: Gujarat, Maharashtra, and Madhya Pradesh. When construction started, NGOs working with *adivasis* and small farmers living along the river began to raise concern about the lack of resettlement and rehabilitation policies for the 100,000 people who would be affected by the dams. Initially, the NBA was not anti-dam but sought to ensure that the people affected by the construction of the dams would be appropriately compensated and rehabilitated.

Due to their mobilization and pressure, the government announced a resettlement and rehabilitation package in 1987. Many of those working with the *adivasis* welcomed the package but by then the NBA had become anti-dam due to environmental concerns and mobilized transnationally to prevent the construction of the dams. This led to a split in the left coalition of NGOs that were mobilizing on behalf of the people affected by it. But their mobilization, nonetheless, led the World Bank to withdraw its funding from the project in 1993. The Indian and the three state governments, however, continued the project without that funding. Many of the movement organizations, NGOs, and advocacy and research centers that emerged during this time continue to exist and, along with the journalists and academics who were active in NBA, constitute the translocal field of protest in Gujarat.

In the meantime, the pro-dam Narmada movement had mobilized consensus for the dams, seeing them as the state's lifeline and road to prosperity, and defined the NBA activists as traitors, non-Gujaratis[6] who did not want Gujarat to prosper. As Mehta (2011) shows, this consensus was achieved through the articulation of a coercive nativism that allowed no disagreement or dissent. The Narmada consensus, she argues, shaped other debates, specifically about Hindus and Muslims, and consolidated a consensus around Hindutva politics, "which envisions Gujarat (and India) as essentially a Hindu polity where Muslims and other minorities would be second-class citizens" (Mehta, 2011: 53).

Whereas both Congress and BJP were pro-dam, it was BJP who fostered this coercive nativism, given Congress's image as pro-minorities, and based on this BJP came to power for the first time in 1995. Dhattiwala and Briggs (2012) have argued that the anti-Muslim pogrom of 2002 was an electoral strategy of the BJP to consolidate power, as these riots usually took place in districts where BJP support was tenuous.

Having consolidated a political victory, the BJP used the economic reforms to chart the neoliberalization of Gujarat. Land was used as the major vehicle for this (Simpson and Kapadia, 2010; Sud, 2010; Yagnik and Sheth,

2005). In colonial and post-colonial Gujarat there were safeguards to ensure that land remained in the hands of the tillers and did not become a vehicle for speculation by absentee landlords and developers. Two such provisions were a ban on selling agricultural land to those living beyond eight kilometers (kms) of it and a cumbersome process, requiring the signature of the chief administrative officer of the district, to permit the use of agricultural land for non-agricultural purposes. In 1988 the eight-kilometers rule was revoked and in 1995 the process to convert land for non-agricultural use was simplified.

This did not lead to a free market in land, but rather to a "business-friendly" process of liberalization (Kohli, 2006; cited by Sud, 2010). As Levien (2014) has argued, the demand for land and fierce competition for investment have resulted in the state expanding its role as a land broker for private capital, in the process dispossessing the poor of their land. Additionally, the state bureaucrats have expanded their rent-seeking behaviors. As one industrialist told Sinha (2005: 228), the corruption in Gujarat is transparent, predictable, and consistent: "Land, water, and power concessions, not to mention environmental clearances are hassle free if one has the right political connections."

While Modi has sold himself as the architect of Gujarat's development, as Gupta (2011) noted, that is "telling the wrong story." The economic achievements of Gujarat pre-date Modi. In the 1960s Gujarat ranked eighth in terms of prosperity in the country and has been number three since 1990, well before Modi. As Gupta (2011) adds, "If there was ever a person who reaped what somebody else had sown, then that is Modi." But what has happened under his watch is the increasing displacement of poor people.

Since independence, 2.5 million people, or 5% of the state's population, have been displaced (Shah, Rutten, and Streefkerk, 2002). In the initial decades after independence, most of the displacement was for state-funded irrigation projects, which were seen to contribute to the larger good and in which issues of displacement and rehabilitation were addressed. Hence, even subaltern movements did not protest such displacement (e.g., Levien, 2013). But as private industrialization and mines became the reasons for displacement and economic growth mattered more, less attention was given to issues of equity and justice, and this has led to the "politics of dispossession" in Gujarat and all around the country (Levien, 2013). This displacement not only deprives people of their land and livelihood, but also their knowledge base, which derives from connection to place, culture, and language.

Lobo and Kumar (2009) argue that while some displacement is inevitable, it should not be arbitrary or for private corporations, but based on a true larger good. It should also include the affected communities in the process of resettlement and should be geared towards reducing inequality and enhancing freedom, economic opportunities, and self-respect. In response to the *Narmada Bachao Andolan*, the state inaugurated a new rehabilitation policy in 2006. The new policy, however, still gives the state the absolute authority to define eminent domain, exempts the Ministry of Defense from conducting social impact assessment, and only applies to displacement affecting 400 or more families, which means it does not apply to a majority of displacements, which often involve smaller numbers. The new policy also does not include formation about informed consent, nor does it guarantee employment.

In addition to policy changes, in 2011 the national government finally proposed a new Land Acquisition, Rehabilitation, and Resettlement Bill to replace the colonial-era land act from 1894. As Nielsen (2011) noted, this was meant to address two issues: one of attracting private capital and the other of preventing protests by displaced subaltern groups from gaining momentum. Hence, the bill does include measures such as the need for rehabilitation, of expanding the definition of PAP, more specificity in terms of defining public purpose, stricter limitations on use of irrigated agricultural land, and increased compensation and consent to 80% of the project-affected families. Yet, it still continues to give the state absolute power to define eminent domain and seems to be more about facilitating private interests rather than protecting the displaced subaltern groups. After much contentious debate, the parliament passed the bill on March 10, 2015.

Even as policies remain inadequate, those facing displacement have continued to protest them. Among those are the small farmers in Mahuva *taluka* of Saurashtra, Muslim fishers in Mundra taluka in Kutch, and adivasis in Dharampur taluka in South Gujarat. All protests are foremost about challenging the loss of land and livelihood. But in the process of mobilizing and forging translocal alliances, they have also begun to challenge this model of development and calling for an alternative that includes them. Thus, contrary to Levien (2013), the politics of dispossession are not only about immediate issues of loss.

Women have been at the forefront in all three protests. They have participated in great numbers, spoken out in public hearings, been beaten, and vilified. Yet, they have been marginalized in some spaces of each of the movements, leading to the gendered geography of struggle. It is to these gendered geographies that I turn in the next three chapters.

Notes

1 Gandhi had emphasized decentralized rural development based on *gram swaraj*, or village self-rule, rather than a centralized industrial model.
2 Ironically, Jay Prakash Narayan was inspired by the *Nav Nirman* movement that initially sought to challenge the corruption and price rise in Gujarat but later devolved into violence as criminal elements and political parties undermined it.

3 *Panchayats*, literally a council of five, were traditional bodies of community governance across India.
4 At independence the current state of Gujarat was part of Bombay Presidency, which comprised the current states of Gujarat and Maharashtra. In addition to linguistic grounds, which were the basis of state formation after independence, the Gujarati elite demanded a separate state out of pragmatic concern that national resources funneled into the larger state would go primarily to the southern Marathi part of the state and to the city of Bombay and not to Gujarat.
5 *Harijans*, literally people of god, was the term Gandhi coined to refer to the untouchable castes. Today, this term, seen as patronizing by the communities, has been replaced by *dalit*, or the oppressed.
6 Medha Patkar and Baba Amte, who came to symbolize the NBA, were both from Maharashtra, Gujarat's main rival.

References

Baviskar, Amita. 1995. "Red in Tooth and Claw? Looking for Class in Struggles over Nature." In *Social Movements in India: Poverty, Power, and Politics*, 161–178. Edited by Raka Ray and Mary Fainsod Katzenstein. Lanham: Rowman and Littlefield.

Dhattiwala, Raheel, and Michael Biggs. 2012. "The Political Logic of Ethnic Violence: The Anti-Muslim Pogrom in Gujarat 2002." *Politics and Society* 40(4):483–516.

D'Souza, Radha. 2011. "Three Actors, Two Geographies, One Philosophy: The Straightjacket of Social Movements." In *Social Movements in the Global South: Dispossession, Development, and Resistance*, 227–249. Edited by Sara Motta and Alf Gunvald Nilsen. London: Palgrave.

Frankel, Francine. 2005. *India's Political Economy*. Delhi: Oxford University Press.

Gupta, Akhil, and K. Sivaramakrishnan, (editors). 2010. *The State in India after Liberalization*. London: Routledge.

Gupta, Dipankar. 2011. "Telling the Wrong Story." *The Times of India*. Mumbai, Thursday, October 6, 2011.

Heller, Patrick. 2005. "Reinventing Public Power in the Age of Globalization." In *Social Movements in India: Poverty, Power, and Politics*, 79–106. Edited by Raka Ray and Mary Fainsod Katzenstein. Lanham: Rowman and Littlefield.

Jenkins, Ron, and Anne Marie Goetz. 1999. "Accounts and Accountability: Theoretical Implications of the Right to Information Movement." *Third World Quarterly* 20(3):603–622.

Kohli, Atul. 2009. *Democracy and Development in India: From Socialism to Pro-Business*. New Delhi: Oxford University Press.

Kothari, Rajni. 1989. *Politics and People: In Search of a Humane India, Vol.1*. New Delhi: Ajanta Publications.

Levien, Michael. 2014. "The Land Broker State: Dispossession and Development in Neoliberal India." Paper Presented at the American Sociological Association annual meeting in San Francisco, California, August 16–19.

———. 2013. "The Politics of Dispossession: Theorizing India's "Land Wars."" *Politics and Society* 41(3):351–394.

Lobo, Lancy and Shashikant Kumar. 2009. *Land Acquisition, Displacement, and Resettlement in Gujarat 1947–2004.* New Delhi: Sage.
Manor, James. 2010. "Local Governance." In *The Oxford Companion to Politics in India*, 61–79. Edited by Jayal Niraja Gopal and Pratap Bhanu Mehta. New Delhi: Oxford University Press.
Mehta, Mona. 2011. "A River of No Dissent: Narmada Movement and Coercive Gujarati Nativism." In *Gujarat Beyond Gandhi: Identity, Society, and Conflict*, 43–62. Edited by Nalin Mehta and Mona Mehta. London: Routledge.
Mehta, Nalin and Mona Mehta, editors. 2011. *Gujarat beyond Gandhi: Identity, Society, and Conflict.* London: Routledge.
Mehta, Pratap Bhanu. 2007. "The Rise of Judicial Sovereignty." *Journal of Democracy* 18(2):70–83.
Menon, Nivedita. 2009. "Sexuality, Caste, Governmentality: Contests Over 'Gender' in India." *Feminist Review* 91:94–112
Menon, Nivedita and Aditya Nigam. 2007. *Power and Contestation: India since 1989.* London: Zed Books.
Motta, Sara and Alf Gunvald Nilsen, editors. 2011. *Social Movements in the Global South: Dispossession, Development, and Resistance.* London: Palgrave.
Nielsen, Kenneth. 2011. "Land, Law, Resistance," *Economic and Political Weekly* 46(41):38–40.
Omvedt, Gail. 1993. *Reinventing Revolution: New Social Movements and the Socialist Tradition in India.* Armonk: M. E. Sharpe
Pandey, Mahesh. 2003. *Environmental Public Hearing.* Ahmedabad: Paryavaran Mitra (Centre for Social Justice).
Rajamani Lavanya and Arghya Sengupta. 2010. "The Supreme Court." In *The Oxford Companion to Politics in India*, 80–97. Edited by Jayal Niraja Gopal and Pratap Bhanu Mehta. New York: Oxford University Press.
Ray, Raka and Mary Fainsod Katzenstein, editors. 2005. *Social Movements in India: Poverty, Power, and Politics.* Lanham, MA: Rowman and Littlefield.
Roberts, Alasdair. 2010. "A Great and Revolutionary Law? The First Four Years of India's Right to Information Act." *Public Administration Review* 70(6): 925–933.
Roy, Aruna and Nikhil Dey. 2008. "The Right to Information Act of 2005." In *Social Development Report*, 205–220. New York: Oxford University Press.
———. 1999. "Fighting for the Right to Know in India." Unpublished Paper.
Sanghavi, Nagindas. 2011. "From Navnirman to the anti-Mandal riots: the political trajectory of Gujarat (1974–1985)." In *Gujarat Beyond Gandhi: Identity, Society, and Conflict*, 14–27. Edited by Nalin Mehta and Monal Mehta. London: Routledge.
Sarangi, Prakash. 2012. "Can the Right to Information Help?" *Journal of Democracy* 23(1):149–154.
Shah, Ghanshyam, Mario Rutten, and Hein Streefkerk, editors. 2002. *Development and Deprivation in Gujarat: In Honor of Jan Breman.* New Delhi: Sage.
Sharma, Aradhana. *2008. Logics of Empowerment: Development, Gender, and Governance in Neoliberal India.* Minneapolis: University of Minnesota Press.
Sheth, D.L. 2007. "Micro-movements in India: Towards a New Politics of Participatory Democracy." In *Democratizing Democracy: Beyond the Liberal Democratic Canon*, 3–37. Edited by Boaventura de Sousa Santos. London: Verso.

Simpson, Edward, and Aparna Kapadia, editors. 2010. *The Idea of Gujarat: History, Ethnography and Text.* Hyderabad: Orient BlackSwan.
Sinha, Assema. 2005. *The Regional Roots of Development Politics in India.* Bloomington: Indiana University Press.
Sud, Nikita. 2010. "The Politics of Land in Post-colonial Gujarat." In *The Idea of Gujarat. History, Ethnography and Text,* 120–135. Edited by Edward Simpson and Apana Kapadia. Hyderabad: Orient BlackSwan.
Visvanathan, Shiv and Parmar. 2005. "Life, Life World, and Life Chances: Vulnerability and Survival in Indian Constitutional Law." In *Law and Globalization from Below,* 339–362. Edited by Boaventura De Sousa Santos and Cesar A. Rodriguez-Garavito. Cambridge: Cambridge University Press.
Yagnik, Achyut and Suchitra Sheth. 2005. *The Shaping of Modern Gujarat: Plurality, Hindutva, and Beyond.* New Delhi: Penguin Books.

3 Resisting displacement, challenging exclusion in Nar-Par Adivasi Sangathan[1]

A spontaneously assembled people's court

After lunch on a hot April day in 2011, Sujataben,[2] Kashinathbhai, and I were sitting on a swing in the veranda of the Khadki *ashram*[3] school's guesthouse, by the river Nar, when her mobile phone rang. As she followed up that call with a couple of others, the long veranda became a hive of activity. A couple of the *ashram* school children swept the floor and spread a yellow plastic tarp on the floor for people to sit on. About six beige molded plastic chairs were arranged in a semi-circle near the swing and in front of the tarp. Sujataben told us that some villagers had apprehended four non-*adivasi* men collecting water samples from the river and were bringing them to the school. Soon *adivasi* men began to assemble on the tarp. Just as I was mentally noting the absence of women, a group of about ten women came and joined the men on the tarp.

Shortly after, the four non-*adivasi* men, visibly shaken and confused, were escorted onto the veranda. Sujataben invited them to sit on the chairs and offered them water to drink, a common gesture of hospitality. Kashinathbhai, after greeting them, asked them who they were and why they were collecting water samples. One of the four men spoke on behalf of the others. He said they were from a company called Excel Environ Solutions in Surat, a city about 100 kms away, and had been subcontracted by the National Water Development Agency (NWDA), to collect water samples from rivers with currently existing dams. Before he could continue, the villagers accused them of lying, saying they were digging and collecting soil samples, which were now in their Jeep. Kashinathbhai asked to see their list and after examining it told the four men that the list did not say anything about existing dams and was nothing more than a map with names of villages.

Then he and Sujataben proceeded to tell the four men about the opposition of villagers to the proposed dams, the *yatra* they had undertaken in January, and the pledge they had all taken at the river in Chasmandva never

Resisting displacement 49

Figure 3.1 People's court at Khadki *ashram* school
Source: Author

to allow the construction of any of the dams, even if it meant giving up their lives. As Sujataben was describing the difficult hilly terrain of the area, one of the four men said, "While we were driving around here I was telling my colleague how hard it must be to live here." Even before he finished speaking, a woman responded angrily, "We are happy to be living here, this is our land, we work hard on it." The young man was startled at the woman's response to what he thought was a sympathetic comment.

Sujataben then handed them a folder she had prepared[4] about the protests to the proposed dams, the *yatra*, their petitions to the NWDA, and, most importantly, signed copies of the unanimous resolutions and formal votes passed by the *gram panchayats* in opposition to the construction of the dams. She then told them that the community wanted them to spill the samples they had collected and to tell their supervisor why they were prevented from collecting the samples by the people's struggle against the proposed dams.

The man who had emerged as the spokesperson then expressed his admiration for the people's struggle. He said, like them, he, too, was a villager and understood their connection to their land and hoped that their struggle would be successful. The villagers denounced his support and insisted that in addition to the water samples they should leave behind the soil samples in the Jeep. He swore that the soil samples were not from the area but from another project they had been working on in Maharashtra. The *adivasis* were not convinced. They called him a liar and surrounded the foursome as they got up to leave. Sujataben had to intervene to allow them to spill the water sample and get into their vehicle. Several *adivasi* youth got into the Jeep to escort them out of the area and hitch a ride back to their villages.

This spontaneously organized people's court (see Figure 3.1) illustrates the rhythm of subaltern struggles where such spontaneous events mark otherwise quiescent periods. It also provides a glimpse at the gendered geography in the Sangathan. *Adivasi* women heard about the court and came unbeckoned, not only to bear witness, but also to challenge the outsiders' perception of their lives. It is through such self-assertion that they have challenged their unwitting exclusion at various points in the struggle, as I demonstrate later. I argue that this gendered geography in the Sangathan is a reflection of their movement anchor, the Sarvodaya Parivar Trust (henceforth the Trust), and its work, which did not address gender inequality, as well as its relationship with the local field of protest. The local field of protest is composed primarily of non-governmental organizations (NGOs) that provide services to the *adivasis* rather than work with the communities to address issues of inequality within them. Nonetheless, *adivasi* women's collective experiences of working on development projects in the past, as well as their histories of greater mobility and freedom than caste Hindu women, have enabled them to assert themselves as I show later. I begin, however, by providing a context within which to understand their struggle and assertion.

History of *adivasi* exploitation and resistance in South Gujarat

The seventy-five *adivasi* villages that will be affected by the dams – twenty-four of them will be fully submerged and fifty-one partially – are located in Dharampur *taluka* (district subdivision) of Valsad district, the Dangs district (both in South Gujarat), and the Nasik district of neighboring Maharashtra state. My fieldwork was conducted in the villages in Dharampur where the Sangathan had its origin and where most of the affected villages are located.

The *adivasi* areas of Dharampur and Dangs are hilly and forested with hardwood trees, with many small rivers flowing east to west across the hilly terrain. Dharampur has lost much of its forest cover, while parts of the Dangs are still thickly forested. The hills, forests, and rivers constitute a sacred geography that animates the relationships of the *adivasi* communities to their lands. On this sacred geography are mapped the histories of colonial and post-colonial policies of exploitation and protection of forestlands. Since independence, this combination of protected identities and protected terrain has been a central dynamic that has shaped the lives of *adivasis* all over the country.

Historically, the *adivasi* areas of Dharampur and Dangs were not part of colonial British India. Dharampur was a princely state ruled by Rajput clans, while the Dangs were ruled by *Bhil* (an *adivasi* tribe) chiefs (Hardiman 2006). Living in thickly forested areas, most *adivasis* were peasant farmers who did not own land but practiced shifting cultivation – that is, cultivating a plot of land for a few years and then leaving it fallow and shifting to cultivate another plot – along with relying on forest products such as honey and Mahuva flowers for distilling liquor.

Most *adivasi* villages were well integrated into the economic life outside their areas, primarily as sellers of forest produce, particularly Mahuva flowers, and later as day laborers. Most communities did not cut the trees in their forests, but used branches for fuel and fodder. Some Bhil chiefs and Rajput rulers, however, contracted with outside timber merchants to cut down the trees. As Hardiman (2006) notes, the pre-colonial forest economy was complex and could not be considered "conservationist." For the *adivasis* the forests were sacred but also a means of livelihood and refuge. Moreover, given the vastness of the forests and their relatively non-destructive use of them, *adivasis* did not and could not conceive of them as a scarce resource in need of protection.

The advent of colonial rule was to change this dynamic even though neither of the two areas were under direct colonial rule. Beginning in 1843, colonial officers negotiated treaties with the chiefs and the rulers that first enabled them to cut vast tracts of forests for timber to use in building ships for the British Navy and later sleepers for the railway. This led to a rapid decline in the forests and to the Forest Acts of 1865 and 1878 that prevented most *adivasis* from cultivating forestland and using trees for fuel and fodder. Thus, both the forests and the people who lived in them began to be managed from above, even with coercive means when necessary. The colonial views of forests first as a commodity to be exploited and then a scarce resource to be protected were alien to the *adivasis*. The new restrictions on the use of forestlands rankled not just the ordinary *adivasis* but also the chiefs who felt a loss of control over what they considered their forests. Hence, they encouraged *adivasis* to continue their cultivation of forestland in defiance of the acts. Additionally, beginning in 1907 *adivasis* themselves began a series of attacks on forest officials who turned them into criminals for engaging in their customary livelihood practices.

Beyond such attacks, *adivasis* in the area responded to their increasing exploitation with a series of spiritual movements, notable among them the *Devi* (goddess) movement, which sought to regain *adivasi* autonomy and dignity by changing their lifestyle via practices such as giving up meat and alcohol (e.g., Hardiman 2006). As Lobo (1995) notes, although many of these movements emerged as religious movements, they were a response to their increasing oppression by non-*adivasis*. I noticed contemporary versions of such spiritual movements in the villages that I visited in Dharampur.

Colonial rule was also instrumental in inventing the "primitive" *adivasi* in the late nineteenth century. Shah (2010) describes how British colonial administrators and anthropologists classified them as "primitive tribes" based on a nasal index in which those with the finest noses, primarily upper-caste Hindus, were classified as Aryan descended, whereas those with broader noses, living in forests and hills, as the oldest and lowest groups in India. This invention of the primitive resulted in colonial-era policies to protect them after decades of exploiting their forests. At the same time Christian missionaries working in *adivasi* communities romanticized their cultures as being close to nature and less restrictive than that of caste Hindus and sought to "protect" them. Hardiman (1987) attributes the term *adivasi* itself to the work of missionaries in the 1930s. Most nationalist leaders of the time, and political leaders today, accepted this primitive identity ascribed to the *adivasi* communities.

At independence, the debates within the Constituent Assembly of whether to assimilate the *adivasis* into the "mainstream" or to protect their culture and autonomy reinforced colonial notions of *adivasi* alterity that both romanticized them and saw them as backward, leading to what Skaria (2003) calls the "nationalist time of the primitive." While many Gandhians, nationalist leaders, and scholars sought assimilation, arguing that they were essentially "backward Hindus" (an argument reproduced by Hindu nationalists in the 1990s and today), others, mainly missionaries, were in favor of maintaining their autonomy and slow pace of modernization (Shah 2010).

In the end, borrowing colonial classifications, the assembly identified them as Scheduled Tribes, protected groups eligible for "reservations." This protection established a quota in government employment at national and state levels, state-funded educational institutions, and access to credit for businesses. Furthermore, *adivasi* lands, forests, and water were not only protected, but in the Forest Rights Act of 1987, *adivasis* were seen as the legitimate owners of the forests. This act has been instrumental in enabling *adivasi* communities throughout the country to challenge the state's appropriation of their lands, which has accelerated since the liberalization policies of 1991 in violation of the act.

After independence, along with the state, social reformers and activists worked in *adivasi* areas to both civilize and primitivize them. In Dharampur and Dangs, Gandhians have a long history of activism dating to before independence. Most of this revolved around forming forest and multi-purpose cooperatives to ensure that *adivasis* had access to their forests and were not exploited by outsiders. These cooperatives did temporarily put a halt to the exploitation and improved their material conditions, but they also became bases to garner support for elections and led to many contestations and conflicts (Hardiman 2006).

Kantaben and Harvilasben, along with Dr. Navnitbhai Fojdar who started the trust, came to Dharampur in 1969 as part of Vinoba Bhave's *Sarvodaya* (Welfare of All) movement. Initially the Trust provided health care and subsidized grain and roof tiles and then started two ashram schools and a *khadi* (handspun cotton cloth made popular by Gandhi during the independence struggle) production cooperative. They had been working in Dharampur for nearly four decades when the Sangathan emerged.

Nar-Par Adivasi Sangathan: resisting displacement

The series of events that would lead to the formation of the Nar Par Adivasi Sangathan began in May 2010 when the NWDA came to the area to conduct a topographical survey for the Par-Tapi-Narmada Link Project.[5]

> The objective of the Par-Tapi-Narmada link is to divert the surplus water from the west flowing rivers between the Par & Tapi to water deficit areas in North Gujarat (Saurashtra & Kutch) by substitution. The project proposed to provide enroute irrigation to 0.52 lakh ha[6] and takes over 1.17 lakh ha of Sardar Sarovar Project command and the water thus saved in Narmada main canal can be used to extend irrigation in Saurashtra and Kutch.
> (Government of India, Ministry of Environment & Forests 2009, p. 3)

This was to be accomplished by building seven dams – six of which were to be located in Dharampur and Dangs and one in the Nasik district of Maharashtra – three diversion weirs, six power plants, and a 400-kilometer-long canal, including two tunnels.

The initial feasibility study for this link project was conducted in 2005, so the local communities were aware that a state project was being planned. There was, however, no action in the ensuing years. But when in 2010 state workers began to come again, they realized that the plans might be imminent. So they discussed this among themselves and with the trust activists. Sujataben reached out to two longtime NBA activists, Lakhanbhai and

Anandbhai, who along with Sujataben became the mainstay of the struggle. In 1997, the two NBA activists, along with others, had formed the *Paryavaran Surakhsha Samiti* (Environment Protection Committee, hence forth PSS). Their main focus has been to educate and mobilize *adivasi* communities about environmental issues affecting their lives and livelihood. Hence, they brought decades of experience working on such issues with *adivasi* communities in Gujarat. As Sujataben noted, "I am not a protestor and have never engaged in such activism before but now I had to become one" (Interview April 10, 2011).

The Sangathan was formed to bring together the seventy-five villages that would be affected by the dams and to have an autonomous entity in whose name the struggle would be launched. But it has no formal structure or membership. Sujataben and Kantibhai, a founder and long-time member of the trust; *adivasi* leaders, and non-*adivasi* activists serve as an informal core group who contact village elders, youth, and women leaders, who in turn mobilize people in their villages. Initially, there were village-level committees composed only of men. These committees functioned only for specific purposes, such as planning for the *yatra* or filing petitions. The main strategy used by the Sangathan was to mobilize consensus against the construction of the dams. A united front among all the affected villages was important to ensure that elected village officials and/or leaders would not be corrupted and divide the struggle. This has resulted in vigilance in all the villages to prevent any state-contracted people from entering the area and doing any work related to the dam. In this they have been successful. As of this writing the NWDA has given up conducting the survey, citing opposition of the *adivasi* community. This was achieved by translocal solidarities between the trust, PSS, and various other *dalit* and farmers' movement organizations, as well as legalism from below in the form of education, which is discussed in the next section.

Translating information into political education

On August 9, 2010 Madhavbhai, Keshavbhai, Manoharbhai, Kashinathbhai, and Jayprakashbhai, all male leaders of the *adivasi* community, filed petitions with the NWDA's office in Valsad, the district headquarters. Sujataben and the trust served as intermediaries, but the *adivasis* were the ones who formally made the appeals under the Right to Information (RTI) Act. It was important for the petitioners to be *adivasis*, both for their active participation in the legal process and because *adivasis* and all people "below the poverty line" can gain this information at no cost.

The petitions all follow the same format of first identifying oneself as a member of the *adivasi* village and then posing very specific questions about the project. This format follows both the formal guidelines and a template generated and diffused by the *Narmada Bachao Andolan* (NBA) and other NGOs across the state, what Tilly (2008) would describe as a "modular" modern repertoire. The specificity of the questions reflects the experience of the NBA activists, who during their two-decade-long and still continuing struggle had learned about the legal processes involved in such large infrastructure projects and whose struggle, in turn, had shaped state policies around citizens' rights in such endeavors. Thus, NBA activists' knowledge and experience were crucial to the Sangathan's ability to gain information from the state.

Each petition asked a specific question to garner concrete information that could then be shared with the communities. For example, Madhavbhai's petition asked the NWDA what kind of information was being collected in the survey underway in their village, what kinds of information will be gathered in the future, and the time frame for the completion of the current survey (Chauhan 2010). Keshavbhai's petition asked whether the Environment Impact Assessment (EIA) studies had been started, who would be conducting those studies, the terms of reference of the EIA contract, and when they would be completed (Jhadhav 2010). Kashinathbhai's petition asked for information on displacement and rehabilitation details by village, where the displaced people would be rehabilitated, and the amount of land that those currently with and without land would receive as compensation (Mahla 2010). Jayprakashbhai's letter asked for further details about which villages will be fully and partially submerged, and whose houses and lands will be affected in those villages that will be partially submerged (Mahla 2010). Finally, Manoharbhai asked for a copy of the permission granted by the Ministry of Environments and Forests (MoEF) to go ahead with this project (Pawar 2010). Within a couple of weeks, the NWDA responded to all the queries raised by each of the petitions.

Thus, they learned about the Par-Tapi-Narmada Link Project, the topographical survey that had been conducted in 2005 and the field survey that was currently being conducted, the name of the company that had been contracted to carry out the survey, their terms of reference, a detailed report of the villages that would be affected, the compensation plans, and the expected date of completion (July 2010 for the EIA and December 2011 for the detailed report to the ministry). They were also informed that since this report had not yet been completed, the MoEF had not granted permission for the project. When they learned that the initial feasibility study for the project was conducted in 2005, they asked for the report of that study. In delay tactics common to all bureaucratic procedures, they were first given only one part of the report and they had to petition again to receive the second report (Bhoya 2010).

I was struck by the languages of the petitions. The *adivasi* petitions to the NWDA were all in Gujarati, whereas the responses of the NWDA were in English, reflecting both a literal and metaphorical communication gap between the state and the subaltern communities. Without translators and interpreters, subaltern groups cannot be meaningful citizens. Yet, local bureaucrats and officials view such intermediaries with suspicion and subject them to surveillance and harassment as well as arrests.

Beyond the literal language, the technical language in the petitions and responses require a steep learning curve, from learning about the right to information and the specific article under which to seek information, to the various steps involved in a large-scale infra-structure project, such as EIA and Environment Management Plans, including those for rehabilitation. All this learning occurred collectively in meetings composed mostly of male *adivasi* leaders, Sujataben, and PSS activists. Such ongoing translocal solidarities were key to the Sangathan's struggle. As McFarlane (2009) notes, what is important in such translocal relationships is the labor and materiality of processes that contribute to them.

Although translocal solidarities facilitated gaining legal information, they did not challenge the absence of women from the process of writing petitions or in the various meetings that were held in the Trust offices to prepare the petitions. When I asked about this, activists seemed surprised and noted that it was not an active decision but more one of availability. Kashinathbhai was one of the few *adivasi* leaders who acknowledged that the absence of women from such processes was problematic and that the Sangathan should pay attention to such issues.

Kashinathbhai attributed his sensitivity to women's issues to his "exposure." This English term is widely used in all struggles and refers to the participation of subaltern activists and leaders in workshops, meetings, and exchanges with other movements and NGOs working on similar issues. For example, Kashinathbhai has been to many gatherings of the *Adivasi Ekta Manch* (Forum of Adivasi Unity), a statewide *adivasi* forum that brings together *adivasis* from around the state and country to discuss relevant issues and struggles. Given the gender projects of the state and women's movements, most such exposures have sessions on women's empowerment. Despite such exposure, in practice, ongoing decisions are made primarily by *adivasi* male leaders, Sujataben, Kantibhai, and non-*adivasi* activists from the translocal field of protest.

Despite such inconsistencies, the Trust is committed to an inclusive process. Hence, once they collected the information from the NWDA, they produced a booklet in Gujarati to be shared with the villagers (see Figure 3.2).

Resisting displacement 57

Figure 3.2 Booklet produced by the Sangathan for educating *adivasis* about the dams

What Is the Par-Tapi-Narmada River Link Project?
Nar-Par Adivasi Sangathan
August 2010

Sujataben, Lakhanbhai, and Anandbhai translated and interpreted the information from the NWDA and made it accessible to the community in Gujarati. Thus, the Sangathan, like the other three struggles, is involved in producing knowledge. In this *adivasi* women are included, as I discuss later. Beginning with the history of the project and its cost (estimated in 2003–2004 to be Rs 4,34,657 *crores*[7]), the booklet linked it to the Narmada Sardar Sarovar Dam and the false premises under which that dam was built to provide water for drinking and irrigation when in fact most of it was going to industry and urban areas. It then laid out the rationale for the river

58 *Resisting displacement*

link project; the scarcity/surplus model; and the details of the seven dams that are to be built, their locations, and the villages that would be affected.

Using the same logic of cost/benefit used by the state to justify such projects, the booklet laid out the cost/benefit projections from the NWDA report to challenge its own norms. For example, the ratio of costs/benefit of this link project was Rs.1/1.08 when most states require at least Rs.1/1.5 before undertaking such projects. After describing the true costs of such projects, which in their case included displacement of 14,832 people, as well as environmental costs to all communities along the project, it provided viable alternatives being implemented in Saurashtra, such as small check-dams. It concludes with the resolve of people living along the rivers Nar and Par to oppose the project in one voice and makes the declarations seen in Figures 3.3 and 3.4.

અમારા ગામમાં અમારું રાજ

જળ, જંગલ, જમીન કોના છે ?

અમારા છે, અમારા છે

જાન આપી શું -
જીંદગી નહીં.

જાન આપીશું
જંગલ નહીં.

જાન આપીશું
નદી નહીં.

Figure 3.3 Slogans from the booklet

Our rule in our villages

Who Owns the Water, Land, and Jungles?
We Do, We Do
We will give our lives –
Not our Livelihood.
We will give our lives.
Not Our Jungles.
We will give our Lives
Not our Rivers.

Let the Rivers Flow! Let Them Flow!
Allow us to Live by the River Banks! Allow us to live!
We Want Development, Not Destruction

The booklet thus not only deconstructs the state's rationale and logic for the project, but also proposes alternatives that draw upon the experiences of similar struggles across Gujarat. In fact, many of the claims and slogans articulated in the booklet can also be found in the writings of the NBA and the National Alliance of People's Movements. As Tarrow (2013) notes, repertoires of contentious language also circulate across movements and times even as they undergo change in the process. The booklet was circulated

નદીને વહેવા દો ! વહેવા દો
અમને નદી કિનારે રહેવા દો ! રહેવા દો !
વિકાસ જોઈએ, વિનાશ નહીં

પ્રકાશક :
નાર-પાર આદિવાસી સંગઠન

મુ.પો. ગુંદિયા, તા. ધરમપુર, જી. વલસાડ - ૩૯૬ ૦૫૦

મુદ્રક : જવનીકા પ્રિન્ટર્સ, વડોદરા-૧૮.

Figure 3.4 Slogans from the booklet

60 *Resisting displacement*

widely in the communities and became the basis for political education and mobilizing consensus.[8]

Gendered geography of forging consensus and pledging resistance

From August 2010 when the booklet was produced to January 2011 when the *yatra* took place was a time of intense mobilization. In addition to the trust activists and *adivasi* leaders, activists from *dalit* movements and farmers' organizations in Gujarat participated in these village-to-village campaigns. Such translocal solidarities on an ongoing basis are contributing to shared imaginaries and language of alternative development based on economic, ecological, and social sustainability.

But even as the village campaigns and meetings call for active participation of all *adivasis*, *adivasi* women were often not included. Ansuyaben, an *adivasi* activist and leader, told me how the initial meetings only included men. When she and other women found out about these meetings, they had to confront the *adivasi* men for excluding them. She told them, "If we are all to speak in one voice, then why are we not included? When they began to hold meetings for women as well, so many of us began to come that there was no place for all of us to sit" (Interview April 10, 2011). Yet, she noted how the meetings continued to be in the evenings when it was not convenient for them, as having just returned from the farms, they had to prepare the evening meal. Despite this, in all the villages women continued to attend meetings and make their voices heard. Ansuyaben did so in a particularly telling way when she composed the song for the *yatra*, which I discuss later.

Sujataben described long days that would start at 6 AM and end past midnight during these grueling months of mobilization. In the process, a consensus emerged that they would do whatever it took to prevent the dams from being built. The presence of NBA activists and the experiences of those displaced but not yet rehabilitated crystalized the consensus. The Sangathan then decided to undertake a weeklong *yatra*, through five of the seven areas in which the dams were to be constructed, and end with a mass ceremony to publicly pledge their commitment to preventing the construction of the dams.

To facilitate this work, several *adivasi* youth, including Jayprakashbhai who works as a driver for the Trust, discussed the need for an effective means of communication. Being spread out among seventy-five villages over hilly terrain with inadequate transportation does not lend itself to easy communication or mobilization. Inspired by the women's *mandals (*groups) that were formed in many villages by both state and non-state development projects over the years, they decided to form a youth *mandal*. Another source of inspiration was the state's recent introduction of an emergency service and a phone number, 108, to access this service. Since many of them have mobile phones, they set up a network they called 208. They collected the mobile phone numbers of youth involved in the Sangathan and shared it with each other and activists in the struggle.

Ironically, while inspired by women's groups, they did not include young girls in this network, which did not go unobserved by *adivasi* women. In addition to a means of communication, 208 became a means of monitoring any suspicious activity relating to the dam sites as was evident in the people's court with which I began the chapter. Although women are not part of the network, they usually find out from the men in their families and hence show up at such spontaneous gatherings as they did at the court. Thus, the 208 network, while gendered, has been an effective innovation, though given the terrain and lack of towers, the reception can be very spotty. It was very handy nonetheless in preparing and conducting the *yatra*.

No sooner had the Sangathan decided to undertake the *yatra*, then local bureaucrats and elected officials, along with the police, began to undermine it. Individual activists and local leaders were called into the *taluka* and district offices to abandon the struggle. The police and state leaders questioned the wisdom of challenging the government whose main aim, they claimed, was the welfare of the *adivasis*. They also tried veiled threats and spread rumors about the activists, particularly those from outside, who were seen as disturbing the peace and peaceful *adivasis*.

Hence, when Dhakalbhai, a Sangathan member, went to get permission for the *yatra*, it was denied. On January 2, 2011, the police invited Sangathan activists Jayprakashbhai and Rameshbhai, Anandbhai from PSS, and Sujataben to an unrelated event in a local school to persuade them from following through with the *yatra*. There, Mr. Gupta, the superintendent of the NWDA in Valsad, made a presentation about the Par-Tapi-Narmada Link project, urging the people to allow the government to conduct the necessary survey so that the project could go ahead. He then proceeded to list the villages that would benefit from the project. Rameshbhai, a Sangathan activist and on staff at the trust, quietly pointed out that according to NWDA's own study, those villages would be submerged and people displaced so he did not see how that constituted a benefit. Mr. Gupta was taken aback by this challenge and other pointed questions and abruptly ended the meeting. Following this meeting, Sujataben and Anandbhai held a meeting with *adivasi* leaders to discuss the feasibility of the yatra and the potential risks. The *adivasis* all agreed to proceed with the *yatra* regardless of the risks.

The next day, January 3, 2011, *adivasis* began gathering in Khadki not knowing if they would be allowed to proceed. Yet they were determined: *Hamla chahe Jaisa ho, hath hamara nahi uthega, peir hamara nahi hatega.*

62 *Resisting displacement*

"No matter the attack we will not raise our hands but our feet will not be stopped." On January 4 2011, permission was granted and the *yatra* began in Khadki.[9] On the first two days the *yatra* traversed the villages in the Paikhed dam area. During this time, although there were three vehicles, the people decided to walk. The *yatra* visited nine of the eleven villages that would be submerged by the dam, and in the five villages of Gundiya, Tuterkhed, Khapatia, Rakshashbhuvan, and Avadpada there were large assemblies. In the Chasmandva dam area, nine villages, including two in Maharashtra, would be displaced. In all these villages, small teams of Sangathan members walked and held meetings.

The focus of the meetings was not only sharing information about the dams and the struggle to prevent their construction, but also to highlight how the state was infringing on their rights as citizens. For example, by the state's own laws, not only do local people have to be informed of any development project the state undertakes in their area, but it cannot proceed without the consent of the elected village councils. In the case of the dams, both the people and their village councils were kept in the dark and despite repeated requests, the NWDA had not met with the people to be affected by the dam. Between 70 and 200 people participated in the whole *yatra* and despite the cold, with temperatures at night dropping to 4 or 5 degrees Centigrade, the enthusiasm was not dampened. They often slept outside on the porches of mud dwellings.

In the Dangs, instead of huge meetings, the *yatra* undertook door-to-door campaigning and small neighborhood gatherings, as the local officials prevented them from holding large rallies. The villages in the Dangs have greater ecological diversity and are more fertile than those in Dharampur. As a result, some *adivasis* are more prosperous from production of cash crops such as cashews, mangoes, and vegetables. Even in such a productive area, 12% of villages were to be submerged.

In total, the *yatra* travelled to forty-five villages: eight villages in the Delwad dam area on Purna river, eleven villages of the Dabdar dam on Khapri river, nine villages of the Chikkar dam on Ambika river, and eight villages of Chasmandva dam on Tan river. It held thirteen large rallies and engaged thousands of villagers through small meetings and door-to-door campaigns. In every village the *yatra* was greeted with *adivasi* music and garlands. People collected grains and vegetables to feed the *yatris* and provided transportation. Given the vast areas through which the *yatra* travelled, transportation was essential. Since there are very few state buses in the area, each village has a fleet of privately owned vans that provide low-cost transportation

On the last day of the yatra, January 10 2011, Kantibhai said it seemed as though every vehicle in the area was headed to Chasmandva village. About

3,000 people, of whom 60% were women, gathered for the last rally. Many elected officials from *taluka* and district levels spoke at the rally in support of the struggle. Very few of them were women. The keynote speakers emphasized the need to "link people not the rivers" of the state. As Kantibhai concluded:

> The Struggle which has countless creative, strong and committed women, youth that imagines and implements a 208 organization and that puts aside everything and gives their life to the struggle, elders and leaders who put aside their family and give their life to the struggle, where there are *sarpanchs* who support the struggle and where the truth is on the side of the struggle which is completely non-violent, such a struggle can only be successful. True power is people's power.
> (Bhumiputra 2011, p. 15)

Following this rousing declaration, all the assembled folks walked to the river. Everyone took a handful of river water and pledged the following:

> We who reside on the banks of the rivers Par, Nar, Tan, Ambika, Khapri, and Purna with the Tan river as witness on this 10th day of January 2011 pledge that we will not allow the construction of Zari, Mohna Kavchadi, Paikhed, Chasmandva, Chikkar, Dabdar, and Kelwan dams. For this reason together we all pledge that we will put all our strength in this struggle, and if necessary will give our lives but will ensure that all these river mothers can continue to flow freely.
> (Bhumiputra 2011, p. 15)

Four months after the *yatra*, when I visited the villages, people still recounted with enthusiasm the pledge and how that has enabled them to keep the state at bay. Women also recounted their contributions, including the song written by Ansuyaben that I discuss in the next section.

Challenging the gendered geographies

> Par bai . . . Nar bai . . .[10]
> We will not let you build a dam in Paikhed village
> We were born here, our land is here, we will not leave it
> We will not let you build a dam on Nar river
>
> Nar bai . . . Par bai . . .
> We are residents here how can we go to a far away country?
> No one should try and forcibly move us from here

64 *Resisting displacement*

> Nar bai ... Par bai ...
> Women's Strength Organization is not afraid
> Whatever happens we are ready to fight
>
> Nar bai ... Par bai ...
> If a big official comes here
> We will give him a strong answer
> Nar bai-Par bai ...
>
> Ansuya Padvi
(A sister who will be affected by Paikhed dam)
(Bhumiputra 2011: 15)

Although the song appears in Gujarati script, it is in Marathi. In recalling how she came to write the song, Ansuyaben recalled: "Sujataben had asked us to write a song for the *yatra*. So one day I just sat down and wrote it within half an hour and then thought this is pretty good. But to make sure, I discussed it with my husband and he too felt it was really good. Now I ask myself the question how did I write this?" (Interview April 12, 2011). How did she come to write this song? In his analysis of women's movement practices in the Afro-Caribbean movement in Colombia, Escobar (2008) notes that women's work alerts us to a different style of theorizing that anchors "their inquiries in a shared political project" (Escobar 2008: 246). Osterweil (2012) similarly describes songs and other texts produced in social movements as theoretical practices. Ansuyaben's song, then, is a theoretical response that emerged from the struggle.

Starting from the chorus and the very first line, the song is grounded in the lives of women who live on the rivers Nar and Par and their opposition to the construction of the Paikhed dam. It then establishes their claims to the land and river based on birth, residency, and national identity. As the song notes: we were born here, our land is here, we live and work here so how can we go to a far-away country? Thus, being moved away from their land is tantamount to being sent to a foreign country. Although many *adivasis* routinely migrate for employment to the towns of Gujarat and Maharashtra, they return every monsoon to work in their fields.

The most striking stanza is the one that follows the rationale for the protest. In it Ansuyaben foregrounds the strength of the women's organization that will resist any attempt to move them, especially coercive ones. The women's organization that Ansuyaben is referring to no longer exists, but was formed almost two decades earlier under a project of the *Bharatiya* (Indian) Agro-Industries Foundation (BAIF). BAIF was started in 1967 by a disciple of Mahatma Gandhi to promote sustainable rural livelihood through natural resource management, including watershed development, agro-horti-forestry, and goat husbandry as income generation activities (www.baif.org.in). In the 1980s, when women became the targets of many governmental and non-governmental development programs, BAIF, too, began to focus on women's empowerment and ecological sustainability. It was at this time that they began to work in the Dharampur area in 1982.

The project they initiated in the area was the development of multi-purpose orchards on small plots of about four tenths of an acre, as most families in the area own between 0.04 and 1 acres of land. These orchards were irrigated by rainwater captured through *bunds* (small earthen dams) and grew drought-resistant fruits such as mangoes, cashews, guava, and custard apples. Vegetables were grown between the fruit trees, and the border of the orchard was planted with trees that could be used for fuel and fodder and prevent soil erosion. The project was funded for about five years, and although one can still see the orchards and fruit trees, the linkages to food processing plants and marketing that were to be established did not materialize. But what the BAIF project did leave behind was a group of empowered women.

When I went to Ansuyaben's house, within minutes about fifteen women who had worked together on BAIF projects gathered on the porch. They wanted to recount their struggles. Ansuyaben remarked on how before they got involved in BAIF they would not even give water to strangers, much less speak to them. She recounted how initially they did not trust BAIF. But as they got to know the people and saw that they were giving them fruit saplings, they overcame their fears and began to work with them. The local BAIF field officer worked hard to gain their trust. Initially, six women decided to set aside a plot on their land to try out this multi-purpose orchard. Soon, over twenty-three women joined the project. Over time, the women also created nurseries to grow their own fruit trees. They worked in teams of ten women, and the first year they made Rs 10,000 each from selling fruit. They also experimented with earthworm farming and compost and increased their earnings to over Rs. 21,000 each.

Within three years the project came to an end. The women, however, used what they had learned about growing native varieties to grow *nagli*, a type of millet, on their fields. Ansuyaben recounted proudly that while there were many such women's groups in the surrounding villages, they were number one. They all worked and traveled together to monthly meetings of the BAIF villages. Given the once-a-day bus service, they often walked long distances to attend the meetings. At the annual meeting of the various BAIF groups, they won awards two years in a row for being the most productive. With the end of the project, all this activity came to a halt. But the solidarity that the women built continues today, and this long-ago women's group is what Ansuyaben was referring to in the song.

Alluding to a women's organization from decades ago reminds everyone of women's strength and is a rebuke of the current struggle for relying on women yet not including them in meetings. They consistently challenged the Sangathan leaders for excluding them, and twenty-seven women from Khapatia, Ansuyaben's village, participated in the *yatra* for three days. They also challenged their exclusion from the 208 network. In the absence of a women's movement organization (WMO) in the area, it was up to the women to assert themselves.

At forty-five, Ansuyaben is one of the few *adivasi* women of her age who has some formal education. She has been active not only in challenging women's exclusion from the struggle, but has also challenged some social norms of the *adivasi* community. Among them was the practice of wearing a half-sari, which goes up to the knees and is tucked between the legs, making it easier to work in the fields but also marks them as *adivasis*. When she and others in her village got involved in BAIF and traveled to meetings, they began wearing the full sari like caste Hindu women. They were harassed by men and women in their communities for putting on airs and acting like "teachers and doctors," the only other women who wore full saris before them. But they persisted, and now many wear the full sari even in their own villages, though it is still not a common practice.

Thus, in challenging their exclusions, *adivasi* women draw upon a variety of sources, including their participation in NGO-run development projects. And they continue their activism through participation in translocal struggles such as those organized by the Adivasi Ekta Manch (Forum of Adivasi Unity), a statewide *adivasi* organization. When I returned in 2013, their struggle had been quiet, as there was no activity on the dam front. But they knew of the struggle in Rampipla, in North Gujarat, against tourist development that would displace *adivasis* near the Sardar Sarovar dam, about 250 kms away from them. They had gone there to join in the *padyatra* protesting that development. Due to the rains, however, the *padyatra* was cancelled but the rally was held, and Ansuyaben, along with other *adivasi* activists, spoke at the rally and sang a song she had composed for the occasion:

> *Adivasis* let's organize and fight this obstacle.
> Jungle mother, land mother, neither is ours now,
> *Adivasis* let's organize and fight this obstacle.

She also told them how the women in her area had challenged the men who excluded them at first, but once they began coming to the meetings, the men had "no class" against the women. She noted how in the Narmada district the women were not as organized as they were.

Despite such activism of *adivasi* women, why was there no space for them in the day-to-day work of the Sangathan? To understand that, I now turn to the trust, which is the anchor for the struggle and the local field of protest in Dharampur.

Sarvodaya Parivar Trust and the local field of protest

As noted earlier, the Trust began in 1969 when Kantaben and Harvilasben came to Dharampur as part of Vinoba Bhave's *Sarvodaya* (Welfare of All) movement. Vinoba Bhave, a close associate of Mahatma Gandhi, founded the *Sarvodaya* movement to continue Gandhi's work after independence. At the time, his main focus was on voluntary land redistribution by landlords through *bhoodan*, the gift of land (Bhave 1964). He did not have much confidence in the state's land reform programs and hence mobilized hundreds of thousands of volunteers across the country to convince landowners to voluntarily give up land to landless villagers. The movement lasted several decades after independence, and continues in a modified version even today, but did not result in any significant land redistribution (Tilak 1985).

In a couple of years, Kantaben and Harvilasben were joined in their work by another young Gandhian, Kantibhai, who worked in the area until his death in 2012, and Dr. Navnitbhai Fojdar. Recognizing that indebtedness resulting from meeting basic needs was a major concern in the villages, they began to address it by providing food grains and roof tiles, initially at no cost and then at highly subsidized rates. These have now become regular programs of the Trust. The work of the Trust is fully supported by private donations, mostly from individual donors. On principle, it takes no funds from the state or funding agencies, domestic or foreign. Shaped by Gandhian ideals of rural self-sufficiency, they also began *khadi* production to provide sustainable livelihoods. Health and education facilities, including the two *ashram* schools at Pinvad and Khadki, similarly emerged as ways of addressing local needs in local spaces.

In response to increased deforestation and droughts, the Trust has also begun a reforestation program through planting native trees as well as fruit trees and building small check dams on rivers to collect rainwater. Thus, for four decades since its inception, the focus of the Trust, like most Gandhian organizations in independent India, had been on such welfare or constructive efforts to "uplift" the *adivasis*. And although women were encouraged to participate in all activities and their mobility and assertiveness are remarked on by all, gender justice has not been a focus of the Trust.

An underlying basis of all the work the Trust undertakes on behalf of *adivasis* has been temperance. Only *adivasis* who pledge to give up alcohol are

68 *Resisting displacement*

eligible to participate in the programs of the Trust. Thus, even as the Trust works to "protect" *adivasi* culture, they are also transforming it in keeping with their Gandhian values. As Hardiman (2006) notes, moderate drinking of Mahuva liquor and palm toddy was a custom enjoyed by *adivasis* on a regular basis and during all life cycle events. Moreover, locally produced liquor provided a nourishing and natural means of relaxation after a hard day of labor. This custom of enjoying in moderation locally produced liquor at almost no cost was replaced during colonial times with costly distilled liquor of no nutritional value produced outside.

During the nationalist period, particularly among the Gandhians, drinking itself came to be seen as impure, and the temperance movement that followed led to prohibition and criminalizing all alcohol consumption. Gujarat continues to be a "dry" state, though as the popular saying goes, in Gandhi's Gujarat, more liquor is sold than milk. Hardiman (2006) notes that in recent years the stigma attached to alcohol among elite and even middle-class Gujaratis is declining and perhaps there will be a sensible return to the history of moderate consumption of locally produced, healthy, and cheap liquor. Among the *adivasis* this ban on alcohol in the Trust elicits mixed responses. Many see the daily toll of drinking on the behavior and livelihoods of families and support the ban for this reason, and others have bought into the moral arguments against drinking. But most *adivasis* who benefit from the Trust programs might still indulge in an occasional drink outside the village.

In addition to the Trust, the field of protest in Dharampur consists of Christian missionary organizations, Shrimad Rajchandra *ashram* – whose primary focus is to serve as a meditation and religious retreat for Jains from all around the world, but it also engages in some welfare activities for the *adivasis* – development NGOs such as Action Research in Community Health and Development (ARCH) that, like the Trust, are involved in reform activities, primarily focused on health and rural development, and the Dharampur branch of Astitva, a WMO based in Valsad that primarily focuses on violence against women. So although all the NGOs include women in their work, with the exception of Astitva, none of them focus on women or gender issues in their work.

In Dharampur, the relationships among activists extend to residential spaces as many long-time activists bought several acres of land together to form a campus where they have built houses and live next to each other. Houses in this activist enclave can be bought and sold only to other activists. Thus, there is a dense meshwork of relationships between and among the various organizations and activists in Dharampur. Despite such relationships, given the focus of most NGOs, there is none that is able to influence the trust in terms of gender issues.

In the neighboring Dangs, the terrain of activism is more complex, with radical left and right groups, as well as Christian missionaries. *Adivasi* rights groups, many belonging to the *Adivasi Maha Sabha*, or the Great Adivasi Convention – a collaboration of forty tribal rights groups representing 30,000 people in Gujarat – are also more numerous in Dangs than in Dharampur. These activists are often labeled Maoists or Naxals, as their work contradicts the interests of the paper, tourism, and mining industries that Chief Minister Modi supported in the area. In the last couple of years, two *adivasi* rights activists have been arrested and face charges of sedition, and there is a great deal of surveillance.[11]

Although supportive of activism in the Dangs, given the ideological differences and the difficult terrain, most of the relationships of the Trust activists are with others in the Dharampur area. The field of protest in Dharampur *taluka* has a long history, but is mostly in the form of social welfare and reform, which is consistent with the Trust's own views. Given this, what changed the Trust's focus from what they describe as "constructive work" to protest was what Kantibhai called the very survival of *adivasi* communities facing submersion by the construction of the dams.

But beyond taking on the protests against the dams, the Trust has not changed the tenor of its overall work in the area. Moreover, with the death of Kantibhai in 2012, the new president of the Trust, a teacher who lives in Ahmedabad and comes to Dharampur every few months, the Trust is itself in transition. This has led to some tensions between the Trust and the *adivasi* communities. For example, one of their private donors had provided funds for a social worker, a van, and space in a village to support health and education for children and micro-credit for women. But a year later, the donors were not happy with the progress and so decided to rescind the funds. The community was not happy with the decision and wanted the Trust to intervene with the donor. The new staff member, temporarily filling in the void left by Kantibhai's death, did not feel it was the Trust's place to question a donor's decision.

Thus, the ideology and work of the Trust, reinforced by the local field of protest in Dharampur, has shaped a reformist activism that reproduces gendered geographies in the struggle, leaving it to *adivasi* women to assert themselves.

Whither the struggle?

At the end of our conversation, Mr. Gupta, the superintendent of the NWDA office in Valsad, made two telling comments. He said it was short sighted of the *adivasis* to prevent the NWDA from undertaking the survey. For if they change their minds in the future, they would have the report ready to

70 *Resisting displacement*

be dusted off and used. For even when the decision is made to proceed with a project, it takes years to acquire the land and for the project to be completed. Then, in an apparent reversal, he said, in general the way that land is acquired for such projects is highly unfair. So to ensure that people's rights are not violated, the process should be more transparent and democratic, and such displacements should be undertaken only when there are no alternatives. He then cited the case of the Nirma cement factory, the subject of the next chapter. This factory, he felt, should be relocated to another site, as there is no rationale for building it in that specific place, particularly in the midst of irrigated, productive wetlands. Dams, by contrast, he said cannot be so easily relocated, as they can only be built where the rivers and topography make it feasible.

He was thus highlighting two major factors that represent both an impediment and the potential for subaltern struggles. For one thing, the changing economic calculus might change *adivasis'* perceptions. In the face of precarious livelihoods and few viable options, the *adivasis* might be forced to reconsider their resistance. Already, migration to towns and deeper integration into the outside economy shape the aspirations of young *adivasis*, some of whom in the future might opt for monetary compensation for their small and marginally productive land. Such divisions among villagers, what Levien (2013) describes as the bargainers versus the barricaders, are not uncommon in other areas where some have sold their land to the state or private corporations, thus increasing the pressure on the others.

Currently, all the villagers are united in their opposition. But this may not always be the case. As Sujataben noted when we met again in 2013, like other groups, *adivasis* do not have a single ideological position for or against development. They are opposed to development that threatens their livelihoods and land, but welcome development that brings them a better quality of life through health, education, and technology like the mobile phone and computers. Similarly, most want to hold on to a sense of cultural autonomy and identity, but they also incorporate aspects of Hindu identities they encounter. As Shah (2010) notes of *adivasis* in Chattisgarh, a predominantly *adivasi* state in Eastern India, the urban *adivasi* activists often have an agenda at odds with rural *adivasis* who have a more pragmatic rather than an ideological stance. For example, the new president of the Trust, a non-*adivasi* Gandhian activist from Ahmedabad, said that he would prefer not to include computer literacy in their schools as the literate *adivasi* children will not stay in the villages.

The second factor that Mr. Gupta noted, which holds more promise for subaltern struggles, is the ways in which earlier struggles have brought home the unfairness of the displacement process, at least to some politicians and bureaucrats, as well as to citizens throughout the country. Although the state and private corporations continue to act with impunity, there is simultaneously a recognition of the rights of subaltern groups. Struggles such as the NBA and those of the Sangathan have contributed to this realization. In particular, ongoing translocal solidarities among subaltern struggles, even with those like the NBA that were not fully successful, are important in two ways. First, they enable active citizenship of the communities through sharing collective and critical practices – such as using legalism from below, political education and inclusion of subaltern communities, organizing *yatras* and public campaigns – and second in articulating elements of an alternative development.

But the struggle also highlights the fault lines of gender even where women are militant and challenge their exclusions in subtle ways, such as through a song, and more overtly through voicing opposition and being present to bear witness. Without specific attention to gender issues, gender inequalities remain unaddressed in struggles for social justice. But as others have noted (e.g., Sharma 2008), women's participation in state and non-state development projects, no matter how disciplining, market driven, and short term, leaves behind traces of empowerment that subaltern women draw upon, even decades later, to assert themselves and challenge the gendered geographies of particular struggles.

Notes

1 The Sangathan is also known as the Par-Purna Adivasi Sangathan to include the river Purna as well.
2 Sujataben is a Gandhian activist who runs the Khadki ashram school and related projects of the trust. Kashinathbhai is an *adivasi* elder and activist in the Sanghathan. The Nar Par river area is on the border of Gujarat and Maharashtra, and the language spoken by most *adivasis* is a mix of Gujarati and Marathi.
3 *Ashram*, or spiritual retreat, schools are usually state-run boarding schools for *adivasi* children. This one, along with another in Pinvad, is run by the Trust.
4 She had on hand several copies of this folder for such unanticipated events.
5 For the history and logic behind the Par-Tapi Link project, see the appendix.
6 A lakh is a unit of measure indicating 100,000. Ha refers to hectares; one hectare equals 2.47 acres.
7 A crore is a unit of measure representing 10 million.
8 A measure of the effectiveness of this booklet was that when I visited the villages in the Paikhed Dam area between May and June 2011, many villagers incorporated that information in their conversations about the project.
9 The *yatra* had taken place before I began my fieldwork, so the discussion is based on interviews and documents.
10 Nar bai, woman from Nar river; Par Bai, woman from Par river
11 I experienced this surveillance firsthand when I received a visit at my mother's house in Valsad from a woman officer of the Central Bureau of Intelligence's Valsad office. Calling the encounter a chat and side-stepping my questions, she proceeded to tell me that her job was to gather intelligence about local

politics for the central government. She went on to tell me how NGOs, particularly the Christian ones funded by the United States, sought funds under false pretexts and rarely used them for *adivasi* welfare. As an *adivasi* herself, she claimed to be committed to *adivasi* welfare (a claim later verified by others in the area) and asked if I was helping the *adivasis*. I told her that as an activist scholar my job was to learn from the people and support their struggle. When I described my feminist work, she talked of her own efforts to build a house in her own name and to juggle wanting a promotion and move with her family's interests.

References

Bhave, Vinoba. 1964. *Revolutionary Sarvodaya: a Philosophy for the Remaking of Man.* Bombay: Bharatiya Vidya Bhavan.

Bhumiputra. 2011. *Par-Purna Adivasi Sangathan Yatra.* January Edition.

Escobar, Arturo. 2008. *Territories of Difference: Place, Movement, Life,* Redes. Durham: Duke University Press.

Hardiman, David. 2006. *Histories for the Subordinated.* Delhi: Permanent Black.

_____. 1987. *The Coming of the Devi: Adivasi Assertion in Western India.* Delhi: Oxford University Press.

Levien, Michael. 2013. "The Politics of Dispossession: Theorizing India's "Land Wars."" *Politics and Society* 41(3):351–394.

Lobo, Lucy. 2002. "Adivasis, Hindutva and Post-Godhra Riots in Gujarat." *Economic and Political Weekly* 37(48):4844–4849

_____. 1995. "Religious Movements Among Tribals of Gujarat." In *State, Development, and Alternatives,* 51–70. A Report, Centre for Social Studies, Surat

McFarlane, Colin. 2009. "Translocal Assemblages: Space, Power, and Social Movements." *Geofroum* 40:561–567.

Osterweil, Michal. 2012. "Theoretical-Practice: Il Movimento dei Movimenti and (Re)inventing the Political." Unpublished manuscript.

Shah, Alpa. 2010. *In the Shadows of the State: Indigenous Politics, Environmentalism, and Insurgency in Jharkhand, India.* Durham and London: Duke University Press.

Sharma, Aradhana. 2008. *Logics of Empowerment: Development, Gender, and Governance in Neoliberal India.* Minneapolis: University of Minnesota Press.

Skaria, Ajay. 2003. "Development, Nationalism, and the Time of the Primitive: The Dangs Darbar." In *Regional Modernities: The Cultural Politics of Development in India* 215–236, edited by K. Sivarmakrishnan and A. Agarwal. Stanford: Stanford University Press.

Tarrow, Sidney. 2013. *The Language of Contention: Revolution in Words 1688–2012.* London: Cambridge University Press.

Tilak, Shrinivas. 1985. *The Myth of Sarvodaya: The Study of Vinoba's Concept.* New Delhi: Breakthrough Publication.

Tilly, Charles. 2008. *Contentious Performances.* Cambridge: Cambridge University Press.

Letters, official reports and public documents

Bhoya, Ramesh. 2010. Letter to the General Information Officer, National Water Development Agency, Valsad, dated August 20, 2010.

Chauhan, Madhav. 2010. Letter to the General Information Officer, National Water Development Agency, Valsad, dated August 9, 2010.

Government of India, Ministry of Forests & Environment. 2009. No. J.12011/55./2008-IA.I Letter to Mr. Gupta, Superintending Engineer, National Water Development Agency, Valsad, dated August 6, 2009.

Jhadav, Keshav. 2010. Letter to the General Information Officer, National Water Development Agency, Valsad, dated August 9, 2010.

Mahla, Jayprakash. 2010. Letter to the General Information Officer, National Water Development Agency, Valsad, dated August 9, 2010.

Mahla, Kashinath. 2010. Letter to the General Information Officer, National Water Development Agency, Valsad, dated August 8, 2010.

Pawar, Manohar. 2010. Letter to the General Information Officer, National Water Development Agency, Valsad, dated August 9, 2010.

4 From strategic visibility to marginality in the Mahuva movement

Figure 4.1 Women walking along the highway during the *padyatra*
Source: Author

Jage, jage, Gamda jage!! (Awaken, awaken, villages awaken!!)
Bhage, bhage, Nirma bhage!! (Run away, run away, Nirma, run away!).
Mehnat no rotlo khava dyo khava dyo (Allow us to eat our hard earned bread, allow us to eat)
Azadi adhuri che, Beeji jung chalu che (Freedom is incomplete, the second struggle is on)

About a thousand farmers, nearly half of them women and some 100 teenagers, trek while chanting these slogans (Figure 4.1). They are segregated by gender, carrying flags and banners, and wearing bandanas proclaiming *Jal, Jamin, Jungle Bachao* (save our water, land, and jungle). They sing songs, chat, or walk silently in the March heat on their two-week, 350-kilometer *padyatra* from Doliya village to Gandhinagar, the capital of Gujarat state. The *padyatra* began on March 3 2011, in Doliya village and reached Gandhinagar on March 17 2011.[1] The *padyatra*'s goal was to meet the chief minister and demand that the construction of the Nirma cement factory be stopped so that their fields could continue to be irrigated.

While the meeting with Chief Minister Modi at the conclusion of the *padyatra* was disappointing, during the *padyatra* the Supreme Court of India ruled in favor of the farmers and eventually the Ministry of Environment and Forests revoked Nirma's environmental clearance for misrepresenting its environmental impact in the area and asked it to dismantle the factory. In this chapter I show how legalism from below, in the form of participation in public hearings and truth commissions, as well as filing a legal case, and the translocal solidarities in ongoing and specific protest activities enabled the farmers to succeed. I then chart the specific gendered geographies within the struggle and in the local field of protest.

In particular, I focus on the gendered geographies of the *padyatra* in terms of the actual journey, the rallies and rest stops, its iconography, and of the bicycle *yatra*, a translocal public awareness campaign where subaltern women primarily participated as cooks for the male bicyclists. I argue that such gendered geographies within the Mahuva movement reflect its movement anchors, who are political leaders. As such, they are aware of the strategic importance of mobilizing subaltern women, yet have a limited focus on and understanding of gender inequalities, which are seen as the responsibility of women's movement organizations (WMOs). Thus, it was in Utthan, a local WMO, where subaltern women participated actively around issues of economic and social justice. And it was Ilaben, a prominent feminist leader in the translocal field of protest, who continued to raise issues of violence against women within the struggle.

Translocal solidarities and legalism from below in the Mahuva movement

The Mahuva *taluka* of Saurashtra region is located on the southern coast of peninsular Gujarat. For many decades, only about 10% of the land in the area was arable due to high salinity. As Bharatbhai Shiyal, the *sarpanch* of Dugheri village, recalled, "There was no agriculture here and no employment. Entire villages would migrate to other towns and cities" (Desai, 2014). The ingress of seawater in the area had become such a problem that the government of Gujarat appointed two high-level committees in 1975 and 1978 to investigate the issue, and following their recommendation set up a Salinity Ingress Prevention Cell in its Irrigation Department in 1980. The cell's main focus has been to construct groundwater structures, such as check dams and reservoirs, to control salinity and recharge water.

It was as part of this effort that in the 1990s, along with World Bank funding, the state built four *bandharos* (reservoirs) – Nikol, Malan, Samakhyara, and Kalsar – in Mahuva to neutralize the salinity. The *bandharos* not only checked salinity, but also were a boon to agriculture. Now, nearly all the land in the region is being cultivated. In addition to providing water for irrigation, the reservoirs have led to the emergence of a rich wetland ecosystem, with forty different species of migratory birds descending in the area between November and April every year.

As a result, Mahuva is a fairly prosperous *taluka* with only 3.1% of its population below the poverty line. However, most farmers own small plots of land and although above the poverty line, still live a materially marginal existence. Socially, farmers belong to various lower castes, called "other backward castes" or OBC, in the constitution, the main one being the *Ahirs*, many have benefitted from the state's reservation policies. For example, Dr. Kanubhai Kalsaria, a member of the *Ahir* caste, went on to become a surgeon and came back to serve his community. He was elected to the state assembly and later became the leader of the Mahuva movement. The farmers eat most of what they grow and sell the surplus, especially vegetables, to supplement their incomes. Onions are the main vegetable, which are dehydrated in the many processing plants in the area and are sold all over the country. Along with subsistence farming there has been a shift in cultivation from cereal and pulses to cash crops, especially cotton and peanuts.

What motivated 5,000 families in more than 15 villages in Mahuva *taluka* to engage in a struggle which, by now is nearly seven years long, is the threat to their livelihood: the partial disappearance of a major water source to irrigate their fields. In 2006 the state government sanctioned 3,460 hectares of land to Nirma, a large detergent manufacturer that had diversified into other industries, for limestone mining and another 268 hectares for building a cement factory. The latter was to be built in the submergence area of Samakhyara *bandharo*, the main water source for the farmers, which is specifically prohibited by law. The state and Nirma claimed that "the water body" did not exist and the land, in fact, was a wasteland and hence appropriate for locating a factory.

Nirma was able to make this claim, as the revenue records, for reasons unknown, do not show the full extent of the reservoir. Thus, the crux of the issue was the existence of a water body and the quality of the land that was sanctioned by the state to the corporation. Furthermore, by law, the state cannot sanction any land for any project without the consent of the affected *gram panchayats*. Yet, the practice in most cases in Gujarat and elsewhere has been either to subvert the process entirely or to bribe the *sarpanch* and get his signature without going to the *panchayat* (e.g., Hirway, Kashyap, and Shah 2002; Sinha 2005). Thus, farmers from the villages to be affected by this cement factory and limestone quarry were not formally notified of it. Neither was Kanubhai, their elected representative to the state assembly.

According to some members and the leaders, what launched the struggle was the announcement of the environmental public hearing for September 9, 2008. It was then that the farmers learned that the factory would be built in the submergence area of the Samakhyara *bandharo* in Padhiyarka village (Shah 2011). As noted in Chapter 2, such public hearings became mandatory in 2005 and since then have become a major site for subaltern groups to protest displacement and dispossession. It was in response to this announcement that farmers, especially women, from the villages of Padhiyarka, Vagar, Mathia, Gujarda, Dugheri, Dughada, Nadip, and Kalsar began to mobilize. The information about the public hearing was not widely circulated, but *Pariyavaran Mitra* (Friends of the Environment), an advocacy group in Ahmedabad, had reached out to grassroots groups in the area. Among their main goals is to enable people to understand the social and environmental impacts of industrial activity in their areas and to present their concerns at public hearings. Through their outreach, Kadviben, a subaltern activist in Utthan, and some of the other subaltern women were alerted about it. When they challenged the *sarpanch* of their village for not inviting them to it, they were threatened with violence if they showed up. This just increased the resolve of the farmers, and they went to the hearing even though they were not allowed to speak.

Women in the movement and Ilaben offer an additional account of what initiated the movement. They recount how Nirma had begun to fence off the land and install security guards in preparation for construction around the time of the hearing. This began to concern women, especially after the experience of a young, disabled girl who had followed her sheep into the fenced-in land. She was threatened and chased out by the security guards.

This incident, along with the enclosure of the road to the local school and the crematorium within the fenced-in land, also troubled the communities. They did not like passing through the compound with its armed security men who often were in states of undress, as they lived in temporary shelters in the compound. As a result of these experiences, the farmers approached Kanubhai, their representative and member of the ruling Bharatiya Janata Party (BJP) party that had sanctioned this land.

Thus, the Mahuva movement, as it has come to be called, was not against the cement factory, per se, but against its location in the midst of a reservoir that had transformed the area from one of high salinity and low productivity to a verdant land. Despite such transformations, the state, without consulting the people or the elected representative, sanctioned this productive land to Nirma, citing the area as a wasteland. Given this, Kanubhai expected that this issue would be resolved easily. He found it otherwise as he sought information about the land allotment. In response to his query, the state set up a committee headed by the chief secretary of the state, Mr. S.K. Shelat, and the former collector of Bhavnagar district, known to be pro-business, without any representation from the local community. Not surprisingly, the committee ruled in favor of the state and Nirma, and against the farmers.

The farmers and Kanubhai were astonished at this ruling and the latter, an otherwise by-the-book political leader, knew that he had to fight on behalf of his constituents. They formed the Mahuva *Khetiwadi Paryavaran Bachao Samiti* (Committee to Save Farming and the Environment in Mahuva) and in March 2009 filed a suit with the Gujarat High Court. The case was initially filed by the well-known cause lawyer Bhusanbhai Oza. Later, Girishbhai Patel and Anandbhai Yagnik, other cause lawyers, shepherded the case through the Supreme Court. The ruling also galvanized the translocal field of protest, which came to the assistance of Kanubhai and the farmers. In particular, the Gujarat *Lok Samiti*, (Gujarat People's Committee), a Gandhian organization initiated by Chunnidada[2] Vaidya, played a central role. Three prominent leaders and elders also came to the support of the movement from the beginning.

Chunnidada, as the ninety-four-year-old Gandhian leader is called, had been working on issues of land to the tiller and the Gandhian vision of *gram swaraj* (village self-rule) since independence, and had initiated the Gujarat Lok Samiti in 2004 to further these goals. Despite his age, he had worked tirelessly for the movement since its inception. Ilaben Pathak, a retired English professor and long-time feminist activist in Ahmedabad, was a member of the Gujarat Lok Samiti and also became involved in the struggle. Sanatbhai Mehta, an eighty-year-old self-proclaimed socialist and the former finance minister of the state, concerned about the development policies of the ruling BJP government and the inability or unwillingness of Congress,

From strategic visibility to marginality 79

the opposition party, to provide a critical voice, also became an active supporter of the movement. As one activist noted, the movement provided the two aging male leaders one more opportunity to make a difference.

Additionally, non-governmental organizations (NGOs) like *Pariyavaran Mitra* (Friends of the Environment), an advocacy group based in Ahmedabad; *Charkha* (Spinning Wheel), a development documentation NGO; *Naya Marg* (*New Direction*), a progressive magazine; Gujarat *Khedut Samaj* (Farmers' Society); a farmers' union; and various Gandhian organizations in the state also played an important role by providing a platform to raise awareness of the struggle and supporting it in various ways, including participating in its protests. Thus, the translocal field of protest included elected representatives and legal, environmental, and media NGOs and social movement organizations that supported the Mahuva movement.

In response to the disappointing report of the state-appointed Shelat Committee, the Gujarat Lok Samiti initiated its own truth committee, composed of engineers, farmers, activists, educators, and political leaders. In two days, the committee met over 3,000 villagers to hear their side of how the proposed construction would affect their livelihood. Based on these meetings, they wrote their own report, which questioned the one written by the state committee, which essentially agreed with Nirma's claims of it being a wasteland. Such alternative reports, or knowledge production in and by movements, have also become a key component of struggles across the country. At the same time, Kanubhai began a public awareness campaign in the villages, went on a fast for two weeks at the crematorium, and held meetings to bring attention to the issue. Nirma also stepped up its actions, which included beatings, threats, and arresting villagers under false charges, and filling up the ponds near the reservoir with mud to solidify their claim that the area was a wasteland. In the meantime, the Gujarat High Court also ruled in favor of Nirma. A state minister offered Kanubhai funds for constructing canals from the reservoir to the villages if he agreed not to continue the legal fight in the Supreme Court. The farmers and Kanubhai refused to settle and in April 2010 decided to take their case to the Supreme Court instead.

Additionally, to mark the anniversary of the public hearing at which they were not allowed to participate, on September 6, 2010, Kanubhai, in conjunction with the Gujarat Lok Samiti, organized a farmers' conclave near Doliya village where everyone was encouraged to participate and express their views. The Congress party, along with other political groups and around 3,000 farmers from across the state, came to the gathering. It was while their case was in the Supreme Court that the movement undertook the 350-km long *padyatra* with which I began the chapter. It was during the

80 *From strategic visibility to marginality*

padyatra that the Supreme Court ruled in favor of the farmers and asked the national Ministry of Environment and Forest (MoEF) to send a team to investigate Nirma's claims that there would be no environmental or social damage from the construction of a cement factory.

In May 2011 a team from the MoEF visited Mahuva, and in September 2011 the investigating team ruled that the land allotted to Nirma was indeed a water body with multiple uses and hence a community natural resource, which could therefore not be given to Nirma for the construction of a cement factory (Figure 4.2). In December 2011, the Ministry of Environment and Forest revoked Nirma's environmental clearance certificate and asked it to suspend construction. In response, Nirma appealed to the Gujarat High Court, which ruled that it could approach the National Green Tribunal, the final arbiter in such cases.

Thus, Nirma continues to entangle the movement in legal battles, hoping to alter the decision. Everyone, however, believes that the battle is won, and Nirma has begun dismantling the factory. Yet, in the most recent ruling of June 23, 2013, the Green Tribunal fined the farmers and the Ministry of

Figure 4.2 Nirma factory in the background and the reservoir in the foreground
Source: Author

Environment and Forest Rs. 1 lakh each for "vexatious abuse of process of law" (Times of India June 23, 2013) when they sought to prevent Nirma from further appeals. When I returned to Mahuva in November 2013, there were no new rulings or actions from either party.

The Mahuva movement has thus been cited as the most successful protest movement in Gujarat since the Narmada Bachoa movement and is seen as a challenge to Modi's Gujarat model itself. But what most analysts of the movement overlook is its gendered geography.

Gendered geographies of *yatras*

The Mahuva movement undertook two *yatras*: the *padyatra* in March 2011 to the state capital to pressure the state government to cancel the construction permit to Nirma; and a bicycle *yatra* in September 2011 along the coastline of Saurashtra to raise public awareness of their success in addressing salinity and to promote *gram swaraj* as an alternative to the current development model that favored industrialization over rural development. Most of the same people, subaltern and non-subaltern, participated in both *yatras*, though there were no subaltern women in the bicycle *yatra*.

The padyatra *from Mahuva to Gandhinagar*

The idea of the *padyatra* was first articulated by Chunnidada and organized within a month. It was an immense undertaking, as food and shelter for roughly 1,000 people for fifteen days had to be arranged along the long route. This depended on contributions by local villages, political and farmers' organizations, regional groups like the Gujarat Lok Samiti, and private donors, among whom were diamond merchants mobilized by a diamond merchant brother of Kanubhai. But the cooperation and largesse of the villagers en route was key, as most nights were spent in fields owned by farmers along the route.

The *padyatra* began on March 3 2011, in Doliya village and reached Gandhinagar on March 17 2011, covering a distance of 350 kms. Under the banner of Jal, Jamin, Jungle Bacho, the *padyatra*'s goal was to meet the chief minister in Gandhinagar and demand the cancellation of the permit for the construction of the cement factory. The *yatris*, literally pilgrims but in this case protestors, walked 20 to 30 kms most days, though there were some grueling 40- to 50-kms days as well. While most farmers walked the entire length, there were tractors to ferry those who needed a break from walking and those who were unable to walk the distance. Kanubhai and most of the subaltern farmers (women, men, and teenagers) walked the entire distance.

82 *From strategic visibility to marginality*

Kanubhai is a practitioner of Vipasana meditation and encouraged marchers to engage in this each morning before beginning the walk.

They began each day around 9 AM and stopped for lunch around noon. In between, there were brief breaks for water that were sponsored by local political or social organizations. Sometimes there would be brief rallies at these stops, with Kanubhai and the *yatris* being welcomed and greeted. After lunch everyone rested for a few hours and then around 3 or 4 PM started again and walked until about 7 PM or when they reached the site for the night halt (Figure 4.3). This was the pattern most days. Most brought their own bedding and eating utensils that were transported in the wagons drawn by the accompanying tractors. Lunch and dinner were cooked by volunteers and farmers, both women and men, and sometimes provided by local communities.

The rest stops, following rural gender norms, were segregated not only by gender but also by hierarchy, with the *agevans* (vanguard/leaders) often in separate spaces that had mattresses instead of tarps and were more comfortable. At most rest stops, in addition to meals and a break, there was a rally where local elected officials and other leaders welcomed the

Figure 4.3 Women resting during the *padyatra*
Source: Author

protestors and expressed solidarity for their cause. In addition, movement leaders, usually Kanubhai, Chunnidada, and Kadviben, a subaltern leader, and sometimes Ilaben or Sanatbhai, would also address the rally. As the *padyatra* passed through big towns and cities, the local supporters would swell in numbers and the number of leaders and activists addressing the rallies also increased.

Visibility and voices of subaltern women

I joined the *padyatra* at lunchtime on March 13, 2011, near Vataman village. The lunch site was an open field with a *mandap*, tent, and huge tarps on the field. About a dozen women were sitting in the field and making *bajra* (a millet commonly used in this part of Gujarat) *rotlas* (flat breads) on open fires, while men were cooking *dal* (split peas) and vegetables in huge pots, all under a hot sun (Figure 4.4).

The other *yatris* were at a nearby temple being welcomed by local villagers. The activists with whom I had traveled and I joined them; chanting slogans, we walked back to the *mandap*. Most of the marchers lay down on the

Figure 4.4 Women cooking *rotlas*, flatbread, at a rest stop during the *padyatra*
Source: Author

tarps, men on one side and women on the other, to rest and wait for lunch. *Yatris* lined up for lunch with their own plates and bowls, and I seldom saw any rush or struggle at these long lines.

There was an ambulance that accompanied the *yatris* and served as a mobile dispensary during the rest stops. Fortunately, with the exception of blisters, minor bruises, aches, and pains, no one took seriously ill during the *padyatra*. As Dhammiben noted, "[H]ard manual labor on the farm everyday has made our bodies tough so we get tired at the end of a day of walking but are renewed the next day after a night's sleep" (Interview with Dhammiben, March 13, 2011). Throughout, *yatris* demonstrated what Laine (2011) calls "kineaesthetic empathy" by holding hands, sharing water, food, acting as look-outs as women found screens of bushes along the road to relieve themselves, and massaging aching feet and backs. They demonstrated this empathy not only towards each other, but also others whom they did not know, like me and other activists and journalists, who joined the *padyatra* at various points along the route.

Most of the farmers, both men and women, were dressed in "traditional" regional clothes, that is, white *sherwani* (pants that are gathered and wide around the waist and taper down towards the ankle) and *kedia* (a gathered blouse like a tunic) with a turban for men and women wearing colorful *ghagra* (a gathered skirt) and *choli* (a backless blouse) with a half-sari draped around the skirt. Teenage rural girls, however, wore colorful *salwar-kameez* (tunic and loose pants), which hail from Northern India but have now become ubiquitous markers of modernity with modesty throughout India (e.g., Lukose 2009). It was not possible to bathe and change every day, so whenever there was some body of water available, such as ponds and tanks (cisterns), everyone took an opportunity to bathe and wash their clothes. Women and girls took special care to present themselves festively as they would in a religious *yatra*. Most wore heavy gold jewelry, especially earrings and bangles, and silver anklets. Most older and middle-aged women had tattoos on their necks, hands, and lower arms. This "tradition" was invisible among the younger women.

Walking in the *padyatra*, not surprisingly, was gender segregated. Kanubhai and the men usually walked in the front carrying the Jal Jamin, Jungle Bachao banner, and women and children brought up the rear, walking in twos along the edge of the highway (Figure 4.5).

But this configuration would change with women and children in the lead at the end of the *padyatra* when there were police barricades. Women and children's bodies were thus used as shields to avoid police brutality. Although they all went willingly and with great enthusiasm, they were not involved in the decision making. Mahatma Gandhi also used women and

From strategic visibility to marginality 85

Figure 4.5 Men leading the *yatra*

children to lead marches during the nationalist struggle for similar reasons. Such instrumental use of women's bodies, however, is neither new nor particular to India. Jayawardena (1986) shows this to be the case in many nationalist movements.

Nonetheless, that subaltern farmers were literally taking up space on the national highway was asserting what Bayat (1997) has called the "power of presence."

Moreover, this segregation did not diminish their activism. As Sutton (2007) notes, even as subaltern women embody "patriarchal" feminine norms, they also embody alternative modes in struggle and resistance. While the younger girls were shy, women talked not just to reporters and journalists, but also to the locals they encountered along the way. They would routinely stop at shops along the way to buy water or snacks and talk to the shopkeepers and others gathered there about the *padyatra* and why they were marching for their livelihoods and their land. The fact that most women farmers did not own land did not prevent them from claiming a right to the land. While women have a legal right to property and some NGOs are working on women's right to land, this issue was not raised during any of the speeches that emphasized the need for local ownership and control of land.

Additionally, individual women put their bodies on the line more expressively. Dhammiben from Dugheri village had taken a vow not to wear any footwear until Nirma was gone. She had been walking barefoot for over three years and as a result her feet are blistered and heavily bandaged. When I returned in 2013 I was unable to meet Dhammiben but heard that she had begun to wear footwear since Nirma had begun dismantling the factory. Bodily denials are in keeping with protest repertoires in India as well as a gendered idiom of sacrifice. In Hindu religious traditions, taking vows, including bodily sacrifices such as fasting or giving up certain foods for certain causes, is normative. Fasting, in particular, was popularized by Mahatma Gandhi during the nationalist movement and has remained a popular practice of protest by politicians as well as movement activists and participants.

Dhammiben was inspired by the everyday nature of her embodied protest:

> Our livelihood depends on the reservoirs and our land, and they are taking that away from us. To me walking barefoot every day until Nirma leaves is a daily reminder of the cause for which we are all fighting. Once Nirma leaves our area, I will go to Bagdana (a goddess temple) offer my prayers and thereafter wear my *chappals* (open toed sandals).
> (Interview March 15, 2011)

This did not prevent women from challenging gender norms in some instances. Since many of the villages along the way had Rajput[3] populations, the cultural expressions of welcome were often martial. For example, Kanubhai would be welcomed by offering him a horse ride in the town and presented with a sword. Ilaben talked to Kanubhai about how the sword

From strategic visibility to marginality 87

was not consistent with his non-violence stance and that many women in the *padyatra* did not think it was appropriate for him to accept such tokens. He understood this critique and refused to accept such tokens at other villages. Women thus followed the rural norms of gender segregation as they walked and rested during the *padyatra*. They also, however, presented themselves as active participants by not only chanting slogans and singing, but also discussing their struggle.

In contrast to the women's active participation, their presentation by the movement was not only instrumental and strategic, but also reproduced patriarchal tropes of women as victims or embodying *shakti* (strength). Women's bruised bodies were displayed prominently on one of the tractors and as such became emblematic of the *padyatra* (Figure 4.6). Most media coverage included those pictures in addition to interviews with women who had been beaten. The women whose pictures were on the tractor had agreed to the display and saw it as a way to demonstrate their commitment to the cause.

The captions accompanying the photos read:

On 20 February 2010
During a silent rally, male police officers brutalized women.
In total 49 people were injured. Of these some photos can be seen here.

Figure 4.6 Photos on one of the tractors accompanying the *yatra*

88 *From strategic visibility to marginality*

The other image alongside the bruised women is that of Chunnidada, the veteran Gandhian leader. There are no images of bruised men, though many of them were beaten as well. Thus, only subaltern women's bodies are displayed as victims of police brutality, reinforcing the gender binary in which women are victims and policemen are perpetrators, erasing the victimization of subaltern men. As Sinha (2012) notes, such an a priori assumption of a gender binary fails to take into account the actual work of gender in a specific context. Such a binary assumption of gender informs the male leadership of the movement, as well as many of the subaltern women and men. In this region of Gujarat, *devi* (goddess) worship is dominant and hence women, as incarnations of goddesses, are to be respected and not brutalized. Showing brutality against women, a sacrilege, is a way of shaming and demonstrating the ruthlessness not only of the police, but also of the development model that in a similarly ruthless manner dispossesses the brutalized of their land and livelihood.

This visibility of women's bruised bodies and violence against women by the police is in sharp contrast to the invisibility and silence around violence against women among the farmers' families. Ilaben and Kadviben both noted the endemic nature of violence against women in the villages. Yet, this was not addressed by anyone during the padyatra except on March 8, International Women's Day, when activists from women's NGOs, including Ilaben, were invited to address women's issues. But at other times, there was silence and discomfort even among the teenagers and children.

Ilaben recounted the following episode to demonstrate this (Interview March 30, 2011). One day, during a lunch stop as the *yatris* were resting and Anirudhbhai, who served as the emcee of the *padyatra*, was entertaining everyone, Ilaben asked for the microphone and read an article in that day's paper that involved the court throwing out a case by a man who runs an NGO for men who experience violence by women. He had filed a case in the Gujarat High Court that asked the government to do away with all laws protecting women, as they also perpetrate violence. The judge not only threw out the case, but also fined him for bringing such a frivolous lawsuit. Since he did not have the money for the fine, he went throughout the state trying to raise funds, but was unsuccessful. After reading this, Ilaben said, "Don't you think this is funny?" No one laughed, and Anirudhbhai said, "Oh! Ilaben you are always bringing up such issues." When no one responded, she asked some girls sitting nearby if violence was an issue in their families and most nodded quietly.

The silence around violence against women is particularly striking, as many of the speeches given by leaders and activists, as well as the slogans, focused on violence done to Mother Earth by the development model. Kanubhai would often say, "How can we sell our mother who feeds us and ensures our welfare? How can we be so greedy and forget her largess?" Mother Earth needs protection, but human mothers and girls are left to their own devices and the work of WMOs who address these issues. Despite the silence around violence, subaltern women continued to raise their voices during the *padyatra*.

Analyzing women's resistance in Argentina, Sutton (2007) notes that while women's bodies are visible, their spoken word is not always audible. I found that in the *padyatra*, women's voices were audible, but only in some registers and spaces and not in others. Anirudhbhai, a non-subaltern activist from the Saurashtra Lok Samiti, was the soundtrack of the *padyatra*. The lead sloganeer and cheerleader, he used his bullhorn and lyrical, local accent to rouse everyone to chant slogans and sing. Women more than men and girls were the ones who responded most vigorously to the slogans with which I began this chapter. In addition, women sang songs, some of which they composed spontaneously to honor Kanubhai. Drawing on their folk traditions, these songs praised Kanubhai and his leadership and their commitment to him and their cause. One such song that they sang often was:

Kanubhai ni tukdi Gandhinagar updi	(Kanubhai's group is off to Gandhinagar)
Kanubhai ni tukdi pachi phari ne na juve	(Kanubhai's group will never look back)
Kanubhai ni tukdi Modi ne thar thar darave	(Kanubhai's group will make Modi tremble)

Another song that was also very popular was:

khedut avya kheti ne jeetva	(The farmers have come to win back their fields)
pachu vari vari ne nai juve	(So they will never look back)
khedut ne utara dejo	(Give the farmers a refuge)
khedut chalya kheti ne jitva	(They are walking to win back their fields)
khedut chalya dharti mane jeetva	(Farmers are walking to win back Mother Earth)

pachu vari vari ne nai juve	(They will never look back)
khedut halya bandharan jeetva	(The farmers are off to win the)
gaucharan jeetva	(reservoirs, the grazing lands)
khedut chalya sarovar jeetva	(The farmers are off to win the sea)
khedut pachu vari vari ne nai juve	(They will never look back)

These songs were sung mostly by women. As Shukaitis (2009) notes, such protest songs are important, not always for their content as much as the energies that they generate among the listeners. This song definitely kept up the spirit of the people as they walked in the March heat. This song is based on the structure and rhythm of a popular *bhajan* (hymn). Each line communicates what is at stake but also warns Modi that they will not turn around until victory is theirs, so he'd better be ready to meet their demands.

Women added new verses each day depending on what was happening and combined them with various slogans that they had been chanting. As Chetrit (2013) observes, orality is a form of subaltern agency that emerges from daily life and rituals and thus incorporates these varied elements. This does not make them any less cognitively and discursively sophisticated even though orality is often seen as a lesser form of knowledge in comparison to written knowledge. However,

> [t]he oral is not only about intellectual beliefs, myths, rational or irrational, and representations of lived experience simple or sophisticated but also a powerful semiotic process giving new meanings to multiple and various new social contexts and when necessary deduced inferences and decisions.
>
> (Chetrit 2013: 90)

This is clearly evident in the way subaltern women in the *padyatra* changed the verse to meet the demands of the protest as well as to demonstrate their power and strength.

Although subaltern men also chanted the slogans and sang, they were not as consistent or animated as the women. Thus, contrary to gendered expectations, subaltern women were more vocal in public than men. Most of the subaltern women who were active singers and chanters had either worked with Utthan, participated in local elections on the reserved seats, or were part of state-funded women's empowerment projects. Most of the subaltern men, by contrast, did not have such political experiences, though some worked with local elected officials, including Kanubhai.

Thus, the state and women's movement gender projects have provided subaltern women with opportunities for political activism not available to subaltern men. Singing, chanting, or talking to passersby, subaltern women's voices were raised against the injustices of the system, in contrast to their silence at the rallies.

At most rallies, speeches were given by local leaders, usually men, and by Kanubhai and Chunnidada. The only women who spoke consistently at such rallies were Ilaben and Kadviben. Mallikaben Sarabhai, a well-known artist and activist, came several times during the *padyatra* and spoke, as did several women activists who attended the large rally near Ahmedabad. In general, subaltern farmers, men or women, seldom spoke unless invited by Anirudhbhai or the other male leaders. Although they were invited to speak, they were seldom invited to sit on the platform with the other speakers.

The seating, however, does not reflect gender bias as much as caste, class, and age differences. Subaltern men seldom sat on the platform either, but Ilaben, Mallikaben, and other non-subaltern women would often join the male leaders on the platform. There weren't many attempts to ensure that subaltern men's voices were heard. During the five days that I was present, six subaltern women and no subaltern men spoke. This attention to subaltern women, as I noted earlier, is a product of the state's focus on women's empowerment stemming both from the post-independent women's movements in India, particularly since the 1970s, and the global gender equality regime since 1975, which has highlighted issues of women's inequality. Thus, subaltern women, albeit as tokens, are assured some voice, while subaltern men are unbidden and unheard.

Most of the speeches at the rallies were interactive, and the speakers often posed the same questions. Kadviben's and Ilaben's speeches often began with personal experiences. Kadviben, for example, came to the microphone with a *rotla* (bread) modeled in cement on her head and began by asking the gathering, "Can we eat cement *rotlas*?" The response was, "No we cannot, we need *bajra* (millet)." Then she followed with a narrative about her interaction with the chief minister:

> When Modi came to our village to get votes, he told us that he is our brother and if we had any problems all we had to do is write him a postcard. I have written about thirty or more and am tired of sending them. He hasn't answered a single one.
> (Speech at the Dholera Rally, March 14, 2011)

Everyone booed. They had heard this story before and enjoyed each retelling. As Tilly (2008) notes, like musicians, protestors innovate from the same standards. They emphasized being beaten, the ancestral connection to the land, and how it meant more to them than just a means of livelihood. The only time subaltern women or the leaders invoked gender was when they noted how the hired goons of the company did not even spare women in the violence they perpetrated.

Ilaben drew from a repertoire that emphasized solidarity, linking her work in the Mahuva movement to the work of women's struggles throughout Gujarat. For example, at one of the rallies near Ahmedabad, her organization welcomed the *padyatra* with food packets and drinks, and when she spoke she noted that:

> [w]e have the support of women from all over the state. Many NGOs and activists in Ahmedabad are here, many who have worked with women's issues and issues of livelihoods and agriculture . . . our struggle is part of this larger struggle to stop the destruction that goes by the name of development.
> (Speech at the Sarkej Rally, March 15, 2011)

Her speeches also captured the emotional nuances of the struggle and the meetings. After the unsuccessful meeting with the chief minister at the end of the *padyatra*, with great sadness and tears in her eyes she said:

> I could not believe the lack of empathy he expressed. He has cement not just in his ears but also his heart and when I challenged him to not use the rule of law as an excuse for inaction, he joked and said how I, who fights for women's legal rights, could now ask him to do otherwise. I was in tears to see his complete lack of respect for the people who had walked all this way and instead of welcoming us and hearing us, he said he would provide us buses to go home.
> (Speech at the Gandhinagar Rally, March 17, 2011)

At most rallies, either local leaders or visiting activists and volunteers, including me, were given an opportunity to address the *padyatra*. At one such stop, a well-known regional comedian spoke in support of the *padyatra* but also made sexist jokes such as how lucky Modi, the chief minister, was that he was unmarried and didn't have to contend with a wife and her demands. Such jocular sexism was pervasive even among the activists who are committed to gender equality. Chunnidada would often note the absence of women and urge local leaders not to be "backward" but to bring their women along to participate in the *padyatra*. Women's absence is thus noted, and villagers and local leaders are exhorted to bring women in, but it seems mostly to be seen and only sometimes to be heard.

When the leaders spoke of women, they glorified their strength and their resilience. Among the leaders, Sanatbhai was the one most likely to mention women's activism during his speeches. He often recounted his first experience of militant women in the Pardi Satyagrah in the 1950s in South Gujarat when 50,000 women confronted police who, overwhelmed by the numbers, instead of arresting them simply declared them arrested and released.

> I know their strength. It is not we who are going to bring freedom to these nomadic women, they will be the ones who will free everyone. One moment she is delivering a child in the field and the next moment is back working. Although they are not writers or poets, they make up their own slogans and poems and songs.
> (Speech at the Gandhinagar Rally, March 17, 2011)

But at the same time, Sanatbhai, when confronted with the disappointment of the chief minister's response would give a call to continue the fight by saying, "Don't be demoralized; have you worn bangles to sit and weep? [A common phrase meaning don't act like women.] We shall continue this fight." This, even as women and girls wearing bangles were there fighting for their land.

When I would address the issue of women's large presence in the *padyatra* but not on the rally stage, Chunnidada would point to the token women like Kadviben or Ilaben or indicate the lack of time or say the farmers are not ready for addressing issues of gender equality. Such token and symbolic inclusion also extended to women's issues. For example, on March 8, International Women's Day, speeches at the rallies focused on women's issues, and Ilaben and other activists from Ahmedabad were invited to address the *padyatra*. Violence against women may be addressed on such days, but not as an integral part of the non-violent ethos of the movement. Similarly, land ownership by women and their engagement in decision making at all levels and in all spaces are not seen as important to the movement, which otherwise highlights the need for people's participation in deciding the model of development.

Unlike subaltern women, subaltern teenage girls were not as active. Everyone from the villages immediately affected by the construction of the factory had participated in the *padyatra*, and the schools in these villages were closed for the duration. Only a few people stayed back to look after the animals and the fields, so there were many young children present. At each stop the children and teens would gather together for songs and games that the volunteers played with them. During such sessions it was always the boys who participated enthusiastically and volunteered despite the attempts of the volunteers to call on the girls and ask the boys to give the girls a chance. Most of the young girls I spoke to were very shy and reluctant to speak in public. Such dynamics reveal that unless there are ongoing efforts to encourage girls to participate and speak, big gatherings and *padyatras* are not when they will speak out. As Voss and Williams (2012) note, such capacity building at the local level is the only way to democratize movements and society at large.

In contrast to this strategic visibility in the *padyatra*, women were mostly invisible in the bicycle *yatra*.

Bicycle yatra

The success of the Mahuva movement catapulted Kanubhai to regional and even national prominence. He was a reluctant politician who ran for office only after much persuasion and only to better serve his constituents. So taking the struggle to a larger arena did not come easily to him. Most of his energies were still focused on ensuring that the Nirma factory was dismantled. But given his newfound popularity, one newspaper even called him "Mahuva's Mahatma," he began to think beyond Nirma to the development model itself. What facilitated this transformation were his experiences during the years of the struggle. Two factors were key to this transformation. One was the solidarity and support shown by villagers and activists from other parts of the state struggling around similar issues, and second was the influence of the two leaders, Chunnidada and Sanatbhai. As he encountered other struggles and heard the activists' and villagers' analyses, he was better able to see the connection among the struggles and to the current development model that highlighted industrialization at the expense of agriculture.

This understanding was further informed by the work of Chunnidada, who had since 2004 begun a new campaign around land rights for the poor and begun to revive Gandhi's *gram swaraj* as the answer to the current skewed development in Gujarat. He spelled out this alternative in a widely circulated booklet titled "Who Owns the Natural Resources? Society or Government?" In it he outlined how from ancient times the sages in India have taught that the people own the natural resources, not the government. To ensure this, he exhorts every village *panchayat* to resolve that all the water, land, jungle, and minerals within the limits of the village would remain off limits to outside developers. Then he outlined the need to bring industry to the villages so they become not just the sources of raw materials, but also producers and truly self-sufficient as Gandhi had articulated almost a century ago.

Sanatbhai, as a self-proclaimed socialist, Congress member, and erstwhile finance minister of the state, was also influential in shaping Kanubhai's vision. Through the newsletter that he published and other booklets extolling the Mahuva movement, such as "The Way in Which the Mahuva Seashore Has Been Made Verdant by the Efforts of Dr. Kalsaria, In the Same Way You Too Can Make Your Seashore Verdant," he influenced Kanubhai to think big. As one activist noted confidentially, for the two leaders, it was, perhaps, a last opportunity to leave a legacy and so they jumped on the possibility.

As a result, by the time the *padyatra* ended and Kanubhai engaged in a collective dialogue with other translocal activists, he was convinced of the importance of expanding the struggle to the larger issue of sustainability of agriculture along the coast. To focus on it, they decided to organize a bicycle *yatra* along the entire coast of Saurashtra. The purpose of the cycle *yatra*, as it was commonly called, was to share the success of the Mahuva movement so that others could undertake similar efforts to save their coastlines, and in so doing provide concrete alternatives to the current model of industrial development that saw villages only as land for building factories and power plants. In a booklet produced by Sanatbhai he especially highlighted the methodology of the Gujarat Lok Samiti, which inspired by a Gandhian vision of working with those at the bottom of the hierarchy, organized "those considered backward," rural women, men, and children, through dialogues and discussions in small, village-level, and large regional gatherings and rallies. Such sustained and ongoing engagement is what led to a firm resolve by people to "give up their life but not their land" and also educated them about the long-term unsustainability of the current model of development.

It was to highlight environmental sustainability that Kanubhai chose to use bicycles for this *yatra*. The cycle *yatra* took place from September 11, 2011, to September 22, 2011, and about 200 riders rode nearly 600 kilometers from Wadli town in Mahuva to the city of Jamnagar at the other end of the Saurashtra peninsula.

Each rider contributed Rs. 2000 towards a new bicycle and the remaining Rs. 1000 per bike was donated by a lawyer. There were no women, as most rural women and girls do not ride. When I wondered aloud with the leaders why they chose a mode that would exclude women and girls, their explanation was that the symbolism of the bicycle for sustainability was the most important criterion in their decision making. And while women would not ride, they would still participate at the rallies. More often than not, they participated as cooks, leading Kanubhai to jokingly point out to me that women were not excluded. Thus, unlike the *padyatra*, in the cycle *yatra* women primarily performed the domestic labor of the movement.

The cycle *yatra* traversed 40 to 66 kms a day and stopped at various villages along the way. Like the *padyatra*, there were rallies at rest stops and throughout Kanubhai, and riders would visit local struggles or experiments by local communities to protect their land. While a majority of the riders were from the Mahuva movement, there were contingents from other movements, including *Machimar Adhikar Sangharsh Samiti* (MASS), who rode for some of the days. Local riders also joined in as the cycle *yatra* passed through their villages.

Kanubhai's speeches at the rallies reflected the larger concerns of the model of development. He began to talk about how the process of globalization was responsible for the selling of more and more agricultural land, symbolized as Sita,[4] to national and foreign companies, characterized as Ravanas. He also highlighted how, unlike other producers, farmers do not control the prices of their products, as the government keeps them low to please urban consumers. As a doctor from his hospital who was part of the rally noted, this urban/rural divide overlooks the urban and rural poor, many of whom are landless and so are not included in this *gram swaraj*.

In addition to globalization, Kanubhai and others began to include a critique of industrial agriculture, especially the production of cash crops instead of food grains and chemical fertilizers instead of organic ones, although most farmers in the movements use chemical fertilizers and grow cash crops such as cotton. Bavchandbhai Dhamelia, vice-president of Gujarat Khedut Samaj (Farmers' Society), said that right now he, too, used chemicals, as his choice was between a hungry lion and a drop off the cliff. If he chose to avoid the cliff, that is, environmental ruin, he would be eaten alive by the lion, the market, if he chose to be an organic farmer alone. So the thing to do was to collectively get everyone to move away from the cliff. In the meanwhile, he does grow food grains organically for his own consumption and hopes to encourage others to do so once they see how good they taste.

About thirty subaltern women, most from the Mahuva movement and some from MASS, came to the large rally on the last day, though most in attendance were men. Kadviben, as a recognized subaltern leader, was given an opportunity to address the rally. Subaltern men, however, do not even get such symbolic attention. Thus, in subaltern movements, not only is there a division between the subaltern and non-subaltern activists, but also between subaltern women and men, whereby subaltern men have the least visibility and voice. But although the gendered geography within the Mahuva movement marginalized subaltern women, in the local field of protest, subaltern women had a space to engage in activism.

Gendered geographies beyond the struggle

Many of the subaltern women who participated actively in the Mahuva movement have been active for almost a decade in Utthan, which is based in Ahmedabad but has several offices around the state, including one in Mahuva. Started in 1981 and inspired by the rural university experiment of Professor Mathai of the Indian Institute of Management in Ahmedabad, Utthan's primary focus has been on empowering communities to become self-reliant. Towards that end, they have prioritized enabling sustainable, gender-sensitive processes of development. Hence, mobilizing and educating women to address their issues has been a key strategy.

Among the practices that Utthan has supported and in which Kadviben and others have participated are self-help groups (SHGs). Based on self-organization and management, self-help groups are primarily NGO-, state-, and/or donor-supported efforts that either provide micro-credit to poor women or act as saving societies or as consciousness raising groups (e.g., Sharma 2011). There are over 500 women in Mahuva who participate in Utthan's SHG, which pool women's own resources and provide rotating credit to members rather than micro-credit groups, which borrow from banks and involve interest payments. They are able to lend up to Rs. 10,000 to a woman in need.

Another important avenue of activism for subaltern women is through Utthan's *mahila panchayats*. Originated in 1984 by Action India in the slums of Delhi (www.action-india.org), they are based on traditional *biradari* (community) *panchayats*, all male bodies, which were conflict resolution mechanisms in most Indian communities for centuries. *Mahila panchayats* were an innovation to address issues of violence against women in the community. The principle of the *panchayat* is to have a group of three to five women from the community, trained by social workers and paralegal professionals, work with the perpetrators and victims of violence through a collective process. All aggrieved parties meet with the *mahila panchayat* to discuss the abuse and what can be done to prevent violence. Once they agree on a plan of action, the *panchayat* draws up a contract, which is signed by all parties. A *panchayat* member then follows up with the families, and as someone from the community, she is trusted by both parties. If the follow-up reveals no change, legal or police action can be taken to resolve the issue. This model was so successful in Delhi that Action India began to promote it in other places, and soon the state began supporting it as well (e.g., Magar 2001). Utthan began training and forming *mahila panchayats* in all its district offices, and many subaltern women in Mahuva became involved in them.

Participation in such activism does not confer protection against violence to subaltern activists, however, as I learned on my return visit in 2013. As one of the subaltern activists and I were catching up on the past two years, she mentioned how she was beaten by her husband because of remarks made in the village about her activism in the Mahuva movement.

Her husband often had to hear remarks about her travels away from home while he looked after their shop, which was also supported by her SHG funds. He thus felt that even their livelihood was a result of her work and not his. When Utthan activists learned of this, they immediately took action and talked to her husband to ensure that such violence would not happen again. By contrast, one of the leaders of the Mahuva movement focused on the activist and the need for her to be less aggressive and to not undermine her husband's dignity.

Such responses from the leadership of the movement have made Utthan activists in Mahuva very skeptical of the movement. According to them, it was the subaltern women who really started the struggle and should be seen as the leaders. Although everyone is very supportive of Kanubhai, they also felt that he marginalized women and did not include them in decision making. Utthan activists noted that it was up to them to ensure that women's voices were heard when expert committees came from the Gujarat High Court and the Green Tribunal, as the movement did not include them on their own.

Similarly, they noted that when Kanubhai was beaten, it was women who rushed to protect him, yet when they were beaten up, there was no organized effort to protect them. There were also tensions around the woman chosen to run for the *taluka panchayat* election, who they felt was a front for her husband and not one of the active women in the movement. Without the work that Utthan has been doing in the community through SHG and *mahila panchayats*, subaltern women would not have much space for developing their political and economic agency. Recognizing that working with women alone is not changing gender dynamics, Utthan, like many rural WMOs, is now working with rural men and boys around issues of gender inequality.

Utthan activists also noted how women were being excluded from the workshops that are being planned by the Khedut Samaj around issues of *gram swaraj*, and they have to be the ones to remind Kanubhai and others to include women in such endeavors. Such exclusion of subaltern women from collective dialogues was also evident in the gathering of the Gram Swaraj Samiti (Village Self-Rule Committee) held in Ahmedabad. The purpose of this collective dialogue was to evaluate the *padyatra* and plan the next steps. Yet, no subaltern women or men were invited to this gathering, which nonetheless extolled the participation of subaltern farmers as a key part of its methodology. So, while subaltern women and men are important for public protests and truth commissions, when it comes to charting the strategies of the movement, participation was limited to academics, journalists, young student volunteers, and activists from various movements in Gujarat, only five of whom were women.

It is not that subaltern women and men were excluded from this gathering – it was ostensibly open to everyone – but no effort or attention was paid to their inclusion. This, I argue, is a consequence of the ways in which the leaders of the movement, the movement anchors, understand gender and gender justice.

Movement anchors and gender justice

Ilaben, the longtime feminist leader, explains the gender asymmetry in the movement to be a result of the movement leadership represented by Kanubhai, Chunnidada, and Sanatbhai. She noted that Kanubhai, although committed to his constituents, was neither a movement person nor someone who had risen through the political party. Hence, his political thinking about issues in general and gender in particular was not well developed. Kanubhai admitted as much during one of our many discussions when he explained his loss in the December 2012 elections as the result of his political inexperience.

Kanubhai became inspired by a Gandhian mentor during his medical training and opened his *Sadbhavna* (goodwill towards all) hospital in 1985 to provide affordable medical care to the poor. It was his work and dedication to his community that first brought him to the attention of the BJP. They encouraged him to contest the local state assembly seat on the BJP ticket. He had never considered running for office, but his patients and the local supporters convinced him of the need for an honest and ethical politician to represent them.

The election campaign he fought against a strong Congress party candidate was tough. When he learned that his supporters had stuffed the ballot boxes because Congress supporters had also done that, he went on a fast and said he would rather lose than win unethically. His first victory was in 1998, and since then he served three successive terms until 2012 when he ran as a candidate of his own newly created Sadbhavna party and lost. He also ran for parliamentary elections in April 2014 representing the newly created *Aam Admi* (Common Man) Party and lost as well.

His political skills and analysis have been honed more acutely through his leadership of the Mahuva movement. But even in it his mentors, although skilled political analysts and long-time leaders, have a narrow understanding of gender and women in politics. For example, Chunnidada, who is a committed Gandhian, thinks of gender only in terms of women's participation in protests, but not in terms of their involvement in decision making or their land rights. Similarly, Sanatbhai, a veteran socialist, recognizes the militancy of subaltern women, but is unable to recognize the ways in which they are excluded from ongoing work of the movement and how that reproduces gender inequalities. Ilaben noted that even as an urban, educated, and long-time activist, she is seen and consulted only as a woman's activist and not around general strategies. So the gendered division of labor extends even to feminist leaders in the translocal field of protest.

Similarly, though many of the major women's movement organizations are part of the translocal field of protest, they are not always invited to dialogues around *gram swaraj*, as they are seen as addressing women's issues related to violence and reproduction and not to poverty or land rights. For their part, many WMOs also do not actively engage with such movements, even if they support them, as they do not like the marginalization of women or women's issues so narrowly defined. For example, the Working Group for Women and Land Rights, Gujarat, a network of NGOs working on women's right to land, did not actively participate in the Mahuva movement. They were disappointed that the movement did not prioritize women's land rights or invite women's NGOs working on such issues. Yet, the Working Group for Women's Land Rights also limited their attention to individual women's rights to land and did not think of dispossession as related to that struggle. So, even though I had attended one of their meetings and had told them about the Gram Swaraj Samiti gathering mentioned earlier and encouraged them to attend it to raise the issue of land rights for women farmers, they did not attend, thus perpetuating the gendered division of political labor.

Although many activists in the translocal field of protest noted this gendered geography, not many addressed it with the movement leaders. Rather, one environmental activist blamed feminists for circumscribing women's gender issues to those of violence and not working with the movement around subaltern women's issues of livelihood. As the work of Utthan and other WMOs shows, this is clearly not true, and blaming the feminists again puts the onus on them to address gender issues instead of on movement leaders, thereby reproducing such gendered geographies.

Conclusion

The success of the Mahuva movement has been analyzed in various ways in Gujarat. Anandbhai, the lawyer who represented it in the Supreme Court, does not think that he will see another successful movement like Mahuva in Gujarat in his lifetime. To him, the success of the movement rests on the militancy of the farmers who were defending the gains they had made in the past decade, as well as the shifts in policy and public opinion created by the *Narmada Bachao* movement. Maheshbhai, from Pariyavaran Mitra, suggests that without taking away from the militancy of the people and Kanubhai's leadership, there was also a measure of

Modi's antipathy to Karsanbhai Patel, the owner of Nirma, who had not supported Modi during elections.

Successful as the struggle was, it also highlights the gender fault lines. Subaltern women and men were active from the beginning in mobilizing against the factory. They participated actively in the public hearings, even though they were not allowed to speak and were beaten by the police and the security hired by Nirma. Despite this, they continued their active participation, including walking 350 kms in the *padyatra*. Yet, as I showed earlier, their participation was limited to certain spaces within the movements. Subaltern women were visible in public events such as the *yatra* and rallies, and their oral productions such as songs were used with great visibility; however, they are seldom made central to routine discussions and dialogues in the movement or in translocal spaces such as the collective dialogues. Moreover, when the movement expanded to other issues and locales, such as the critique of the development model around the state, they were completely excluded by the choice of using bicycles as a symbol of self-sufficiency and sustainability, notwithstanding that in rural Gujarat men and boys are the ones most likely to ride bicycles. By contrast, subaltern men were present only as protestors and did not have even as much voice as subaltern women.

This gendered geography of the movement has not, however, limited women's agency. This is in large part due to the ongoing work of WMOs such as Utthan, which has not only mobilized them through SHGs but also actively engaged them in addressing issues of violence in the home, as well as working for political empowerment through the 33% reservation of seats in the *gram panchayats*. Although this has been positive for subaltern women, it has absolved political leaders and movements from addressing women's issues within the struggle and organizing subaltern men. Such outsourcing of women's issues has consequences not only for women's lives in the homes, where they are not safe from violence, but also for movements which fail to develop a gendered perspective on social justice. But some movements like MASS have begun to address this issue, as I discuss in the next chapter

Notes

1 I participated in the *yatra* from March 13–17, 2011.
2 *Dada* means paternal grandfather.
3 Rajputs are people with Rajasthani ancestry. Located at the western entrance of what is today India, their history is one of constant invasions and hence of a fierce martial culture.
4 In the epic Ramayana, Sita, the wife of the Hindu god Ram, was discovered as an infant by a farmer plowing his field. While in exile with Ram, she is abducted by Ravana, the king of Lanka, hence the symbolism.

References

Bayat, Asef. 1997. *Street Politics: Poor People's Movements in Iran.* New York: Columbia University Press.
Chetrit, Joseph. 2013. *Textual Orality and Knowledge of Illiterate Women: The Textual Performance of Jewish Women in Morocco.* London: Routledge.
Desai, Shweta. 2014. "Meet the Bhavnagar Villagers Who are Fighting the Gujarat Model in Court – and Winning." *Scroll.In.* Wednesday, June 18, 2014.
Hirway, Indira, S. P. Kashyap, and Amita Shah, editors. 2002. *Dynamics of Development in Gujarat.* Ahmedabad: Concept Publishing Company.
Jayawardena, Kumari. 1986. *Feminism and Nationalism in the Third World.* London: Zed Books.
Laine, Sofi. 2011. "Grounded Globalizations of Transnational Social Movements: Ethnographic Analysis on Free Hugs Campaign at the World Social Forum Belém 2009!" *Ephemera* 11(3):243–257.
Lukose, Ritty. 2009. *Liberalization's Children: Gender, Youth, and Consumer Citizenship in Globalizing India.* Durham: Duke University Press.
Magar, Veronica. 2001. "Resisting Domestic Violence and Caste Inequality." In *Feminism and Antiracism: International Struggles for Justice.* 37–58. Edited by Twine France and Kathleen Bleed. New York: New York University Press.
Shah, Jumana. 2011. "Village Land Belongs to Us." *DNA*, March 3, 2011.
Sharma, Shubhra. 2011. *"Neoliberalism" as Betrayal: State, Feminism, and a Women's Education Program in India.* London: Palgrave McMillan.
Shukaitis, Stevphen. 2009. *Imaginal Machines: Autonomy & Self-Organization in the Revolutions of Everyday Life.* New York: Autonomedia.
Sinha, Assema. 2005. *The Regional Roots of Development Politics in India.* Bloomington: Indiana University Press.
Sinha, Mrinalini. 2012. "A Global Perspective on Gender: What's South Asia Got to Do with It?" In *South Asian Feminisms.* 356–374. Edited by Ania Loomba and Ritty Lukose. Durham and London: Duke University Press.
Sutton, Barbara. 2007. *"Poner el Cuerpo*: Women's Embodiment and Political Resistance in Argentina." *Latin American Politics and Society*, 49(3):129–162.
Tilly, Charles. 2008. *Contentious Performances.* Cambridge: Cambridge University Press.
Times of India. 2013. "Mahuva Farmers Fined for Opposing Proposed Nirma Cement Plant." June 23.
Voss, Kim and Michelle Williams. 2012. "The Local in the Global: Rethinking Social Movements in the new Millennium." *Democratization*, 19(2):352–377.

5 Ongoing engagement in gender justice in MASS

I live in the ocean, chanting *Allah*'s name and *Prabhu*'s[1] name
I am an ocean fish.
Saheb, you operated a steamboat in our waters, so be it, but why did you dump chemicals in it?
I am an ocean fish.
Saheb, why did you fill our creeks, and bury our livelihoods?
I am an ocean fish.
Why did you cut the mangroves and separate my children from them?
I am ocean fish.
Saheb, why did you come to our piers and bring misery to our sands?
I am an ocean fish.
Saheb, it is OK that you built a jetty but you should not have dumped ashes from it.
It is Ibrahim Lodi's appeal, do not steal my children's livelihood.[2]

Ibrahim Lodi, affectionately called Ibrahimkaka by everyone, is a fisher and respected elder of his community and a leader of *Machimar Adhikar Sangharsh Samiti* (MASS). Inspired by Sufi poetry, he has been composing poems and songs for years, most of them in response to social and political issues facing his community. He wrote this song to protest the Om Prakash Group (OPG) power plant that was to be constructed not far from his village of Bhadreshwar.[3] Written from the perspective of an ocean fish, and by extension the fishers, it emphasizes the destruction wrought by the development of the coastline and urges the sahib, the master, not to steal the livelihood of the next generation of fishers. Since 2009, the fishers have been protesting the construction of the plant, and their protest, along with legalism from below, did result in technological changes in the OPG power plant, though it could not prevent its construction.

Hence, when I arrived in Bhadreshwar in the early morning haze and dust two years after my initial field research in 2011, I barely recognized

104 Ongoing engagement in gender justice

the village, which now had a distinct skyline. The OPG power plant was near completion, and there was another large institutional building next to it, which I later learned was a new school built by the Adani Corporation specifically for fishers' children (Figure 5.1).

In what follows, I analyze how the local and translocal fields of protest not only shaped their protest repertoires, but also their pre-struggle and continuing activism. For many of the fishers, the struggle is not over yet. Tensions and dilemmas have emerged between the fisher activists – who welcome the concessions that their struggle has enabled but are still committed to

Figure 5.1 The OPG power plant under construction in Bhadreshwar, October 2013
Source: Author

the closure of the plant – and the non-fisher activists – who are conflicted about the fishers' unyielding position, which has had several consequences for their immediate well-being, such as better living conditions on the coast and schooling for their children as well as the long-term sustainability of their livelihoods. I also show how MASS's relationship with its movement anchor has led to gender justice work on an ongoing basis, thus avoiding some aspects of the gendered geographies evident in the previous two struggles. Yet, given the gender segregation of most rural spaces, women are not part of the informal discussions and decision making that happen in those gendered spaces, but they are included in the private spaces of collective dialogues and trainings undertaken by MASS in conjunction with other actors in Mundra *taluka*.

The emergence of the nested, local field of protest and the movement anchor

Unlike the previous two struggles in which the subaltern groups mobilized in response to specific threat, the fishers had formed MASS, a registered trade union, in 2008, a year before their struggle against the OPG power plant, and had been organized for six years prior to that by a local non-governmental organization (NGO),[4] the Bhadreshwar *Setu* (bridge, henceforth BSetu). The BSetu was one of thirty-three *Setus* set up as relief centers after the massive earthquake that struck Gujarat in 2001.[5] They were established by the Kutch *Navnirman Abhiyan* (Campaign for the Reconstruction of Kutch, henceforth Abhiyan): a network of thirty-eight development, educational, women's empowerment, and social welfare organizations.[6] Abhiyan itself had emerged in 1998 to coordinate relief efforts after that year's devastating cyclone. It is this relationship among organizations that I describe as a nested, local field of protest.

Following the cyclone relief and rehabilitation work, by 2003 the *Setus* became "human resource centers that could mobilize (the) community to address its everyday as well as long term development concerns" (Setu, n.d.). From their origins in crisis, working with the influx of donors and NGOs, *Setus* have evolved a model of praxis that they believe addresses the limitations of NGOs, donors, and the government – who they believe create dependencies and fail to empower local communities – by building self-governing institutions. Each *Setu* has a team of two to three paid staff members, usually social workers or rural management graduates, who are based in a village that is central to the cluster of fifteen to twenty villages that it supports.

Their work focuses on livelihood, information exchange, and decentralized planning. They work with *panchayats* to develop plans, seek funding, and implement monitoring and audit on the principles of good governance, social justice, and equity. *Gram sabhas*, village *panchayat* meetings, have been used as spaces for dialogue and discussion between the community and its elected leaders. Women and youth groups are specifically targeted and livelihood collectives are mobilized in most *Setus*.[7] As their brochure notes, "SETU intends to alter the mainstream instead of creating alternatives in the existing scenario." While they enable local communities to raise funds and even act as trustees for community funds, they do not fund or implement any activities in the villages.

Setus also work to strengthen communities by building a cadre of six resourceful people within each village: a paralegal, a paraveterinarian, a para-health professional, a para-agriculturalist, a paraengineer, and a community teacher.[8] "The idea is to recognize, articulate & take pride in the internal strengths of a village, nurture them thereby using them to transform the existing shortcomings" (Setu, n.d.). Of the initial thirty-three centers, today there are only eighteen *Setus* that are still functioning, covering 360 villages and sixty hamlets and serving a population of 90,000 people. Together they work with 164 *panchayats* and 1,300 elected members. Despite a common vision and approach, each *Setu* determines its own set of priorities, and that is how the BSetu began to work with fishers and organize them into a union.

But how did a network like Abhiyan, that had come together to provide relief and rehabilitation after a natural disaster, come to engage in such political work and, more importantly, continue it for nearly two decades? One immediate factor was the continuing need for relief and rehabilitation due to three major disasters: the 1998 and 1999 cyclones and then the 2001 earthquake. This meant that there were large funds from national and international sources that continued to pour into the area for many years that supported the Abhiyan infrastructure. The *Setus*, however, also represent the vision and praxis of several activists within Abhiyan who had been radicalized during the 1970s. As noted in Chapter 2, during the 1960s and 1970s, many urban professionals began working in poor urban and rural communities to empower subaltern groups around issues of development but with a commitment to participatory democracy (e.g., Sheth 2007).

Several activists of Abhiyan are outsiders to Kutch but have lived in the area since the late 1980s and have worked with specific groups such as women, youth, and artisans around sustainable livelihoods. They saw this crisis-based coming together of financial and organizational resources as an opportune time to put in place a long-term strategy. As Sushma Ayengar (one of the activists instrumental in this transformation) noted, the natural disasters facilitated the coming together of various social and political actors in the district, and in the process of rehabilitation work, facilitated understanding of the importance of building bridges between local communities, the state, and other actors for more sustained development. Thus, Abhiyan provides a counter example to the common pattern of change in organizational goals from those oriented to change to ones that support organizational maintenance.

Many activists in Kutch attribute the longevity of Abhiyan to the particular geography of Kutch. In addition to being a peninsula and physically separated from mainland Gujarat, since colonial times, the formal history of Kutch linked it culturally to Sindh in Pakistan and saw it as a cross-roads of peoples and ideas along the Indian Ocean trade routes. Hence, it has an autonomous political and cultural identity, which has made it marginal in mainstream Gujarati politics, but created strong bonds among people who live there. Moreover, although Kutch is the largest district in the country, it has two deserts and a challenging terrain and hence is sparsely populated. All these factors have contributed to strong ties among activists of varying political convictions. This, in turn, has meant that they were willing to listen to and be influenced by each other. For example, there are several Jain welfare organizations in the network whose members see fishing as a sinful activity based on their religious beliefs of non-violence. Yet, after learning about the fishers' travails, they have become supporters of their struggle for livelihood.

Like Abhiyan, the eighteen *Setus* that are still active have been resilient because of the work they do in the local communities, as exemplified by BSetu. While the activities of each *Setu* originate with the staff in that office, they are discussed collectively within Abhiyan and hence have the support of the entire network.

Building a participatory and gender-inclusive pre-struggle activism

The work of BSetu was initiated by Bharatbhai Patel,[9] who is no longer employed by BSetu, but continues to live and work there. He was joined by two staff members, Rakeshbhai and Usmanbhai, and they began to work with the fishers, as they were among the most impoverished groups and were facing imminent threats to their livelihood from the rapid industrialization of the coastal *taluka* of Mundra, where Bhadreshwar is located.

> A prominent feature of the Mundra Coast is the vast intertidal zone comprising a network of creeks, estuaries and mudflats. This zone is unique and very important because fishermen use these natural creeks to land their boats to keep them safe from strong winds and currents. The creeks also form a natural drainage system which, if disturbed, can lead to flooding during monsoons.
>
> (Hit *Rakshak Manch* et al., 2013)

Additionally, the coast supports a rich ecosystem of mangroves, coral reefs, and sand dunes.

The fishers in the area are Muslims and unlike other parts of Gujarat have not endured violence at the hands of the local Hindu castes, which range from Rajputs, called *darbars*, to the lower-caste *rabaris*, pastoralists, *Koli* and *Kanbi* Patels, farmers, and *dalits*. The fishers are *pagadiya* (foot fishers), meaning that they primarily use nets and small boats. During the fishing season – from the end of one monsoon to the beginning of the next, roughly nine months from September to June – they live in temporary shelters on the mudflats and dunes called *bandars* (harbors or piers). There are seven such *bandars* in Mundra *taluka* where *pagadiya* fishers fish (Figure 5.2). Typically, the whole family migrates to the coast during the fishing season, yet the temporary settlements have no running water, toilet, or electricity and no schools for the children or medical care for the families. Because of this migration between the coast and their villages, they do not have titles to the coastal land where families have fished for generations, an issue that BSetu and others are trying to address.

At the end of the fishing season, they return to their villages, often at some distance from the *bandars*. More than 1,000 families in the coastal area in Mundra are involved in such fishing. "Besides fishing in high seas, about 229 people are involved in direct vendoring, 73 in net making and repairing, and over 5,000 women in processing the fish (Mundra Hit Rakshak Manch, et al., 2013: 3).

Until the late 1980s, when this part of the coast of Kutch was declared a special economic zone (SEZ) that led to its rapid industrial development, it was a sparsely populated area. The development of infrastructure industries such as ports and thermal power plants saw a large-scale destruction of the second-largest mangroves growth in the country.[10] The Adani Corporation owns the most land and industries in the area, a great majority of which it received at very low cost from the state. Industrialization, with its need for workers, has resulted in a population influx from other states in the country. Thus, from being a place of out-migration and relatively isolated, Kutch has now become home to many peoples and languages from across the country.

Among the first issues that affected the fishers due to this industrialization was losing access to their fishing grounds. Their first struggle was against the construction of an airfield by Adani Corporation that enclosed the road to the *bandar* in Shekhadia. The fishers, supported by BSetu and other legal and environmental advocates in the state, challenged this encroachment on their right of way to the water. Their protests, which sometimes turned violent, along with advocacy work resulted in their retaining their access to the *bandar* through the airfield.

Ongoing engagement in gender justice 109

Figure 5.2 Fisher communities on Randh *bandar*
Source: Author

The support of the BSetu staff during what came to be called the Shekhadia movement earned them the trust of the fishers from the seven *bandars* in Mundra *taluka*. As Usmanbhai, one of the BSetu staff recalls, "[W]hen we first started work in Bhadreshwar, they did not trust us as we were paid staff and so they thought we were just doing our job and not really interested in them or their concerns. So, when we had meetings very few people would come" (Interview with Usmanbhai, February 19, 2011). But this changed after the Shekhadia success. Soon the staff conducted a survey to gain a better understanding of the community. The survey revealed the high indebtedness of the community and their exploitation by the merchants to whom they sold their fish.

Based on these findings Bharatbhai, Rakeshbhai, and Usmanbhai began to organize the fishers in all the seven *bandars*. They did so through two mechanisms: a political one that involved the formation of *bandar panchayats* to give them a voice and an avenue for self-governance; and an economic one, the formation of a producer company that would give them collective power to get better prices for their catch and provide loans to pay off their debts. In both cases, attention was paid to ensure gender parity.

The *bandar panchayats* had an executive body with representation from each *bandar* that had to include both men and women. Given *Setus'* commitment to gender equality, BSetu staff had emphasized involving women from the start. But Rakeshbhai recalled how the fishers themselves came to realize the importance of including women:

> Once we had gone to the District Collector's Office in Bhuj with a petition to ask for basic facilities on the *bandars*. Our past efforts to meet with him had failed. This time we had five women with us. On his way out the Collector saw the women and asked them to come in and asked them how he could help them. What they had been unable to achieve before they were able to this time because of the presence of the women.
> (Interview with Rakeshbhai February 18, 2011)

It allowed Rakeshbhai to explain to them the state's commitment to women's empowerment and how this can help them in their struggles as well. Over the years, the *bandar panchayats* have become inactive, but the practice of including women in deliberations and dialogues continues to inform the work of BSetu.

Along with *bandar panchayats*, BSetu began addressing the fishers' major issues, namely inconsistent prices for the fish and indebtedness. Because of the lack of infrastructure and poverty, most of the catch is dried on the *bandar*, as there are no facilities for transporting fresh fish. Women are the ones who sort and dry the fish (Figure 5.3).

In a survey, BSetu found that most of the fishers owed between Rs. 10,000 and Rs. 100,000. So BSetu decided to work with those in the middle of that range. With the help of Abhiyan, they explored possibilities for raising funds to enable them to pay off their debts and ways of increasing the price of their fish. Working for a year and a half, they were able to get funds through Care India to help twenty fishers pay off their debt. By 2006, BSetu initiated the formation of the Kutch Seafood Producer Company so that fishers could negotiate better prices for their fish. The members of the producer company are families, rather than individuals, and men and women are co-owners in the company. A producer company was a new form of cooperative introduced by legislation in 2002 as part of India's neoliberal reforms to ensure that cooperatives remained competitive. The main frustrations expressed by managers of cooperatives were the cumbersome and archaic legislative aspects of the Registrar of Cooperative Societies, a national body. A producer company is referred to as a new-generation cooperative.

Ongoing engagement in gender justice 111

Figure 5.3 Fish drying at Junna *bandar*
Source: Author

At the core of the design of the "producer company" are its members, who have to be "primary producers," that is, persons engaged in an activity connected with, or related to, primary produce. The design also introduces new systems for accountability and transparency in what are otherwise still community-based organizations committed to "cooperative" values.

(Bhandari, 2010: 2)

Five years later, in 2011, there were 149 members in the company that also owned 100 boats and had a turnover of almost Rs. 2 crores. The price of fish had jumped from around Rs.1800 per ton to Rs. 2800 per ton. Fishers have also improved the quality of the dried fish by training women who sort and dry the fish. But there was also a setback in 2011 when a merchant absconded with over Rs. 15 lakh of their payment and who has still not been found. This resulted in families leaving the company, and the membership declined to only thirty families. Learning from this experience, BSetu sought the help of the South Indian Federation of Fishworkers' Societies in Tamil Nadu, who have a longer and more successful history of such companies, to help them with practices of accountability.

By 2013 the membership had rebounded to 130 families. The company now employs a manager, four staff members, an accountant, an IT person, and staff to look after the storage facility and work on the seven *bandars*. Moreover, in addition to the dried fish that was normally sold by the fishers due to lack of refrigeration facilities, they now catch and sell eight varieties of fresh fish. The producer company is able to contract with refrigerated trucks to enable them to sell fresh fish, which bring a higher price. As one of the staff members from the South Indian Federation noted, moving to fresh fish would free women and children, who do most of the activities related to drying, to pursue other work and education. The main limitation to the continuing growth of the producer company is the lack of capital.

It was during this time that they were contacted by the National Forum of Fishers, which led to the formation of MASS.

The national field of protest and the formation of MASS

The National Forum of Fishers (NFF), the only national federation of state-level small and artisanal fish workers unions (www.nffindia.org), contacted BSetu during its national campaign against changes in the national coastal zone regulation policy. NFF had emerged in the late 1970s as a result of fisher struggles against the increasing privatization and mechanization of fishing in the country. Small and artisanal fishers from South and West India met in Chennai, Tamil Nadu, to seek regulation of fisheries to ensure the sustainability of their livelihood and the environment. They formed the National Forum of Catamaran and Country Boat Fishermen's Rights and Marine Wealth, which later was renamed the NFF. Since its formation, the NFF has focused on mobilizing fishing communities in all the coastal states around fishing policies. In particular, their focus has been the industrial development of the coastline that is threatening the livelihoods of small fishers and the marine ecology.

In 1989, NFF organized a coastal *yatra* in which fishers from the west coast, beginning in Gujarat, and the east coast, starting in West Bengal, converged in the South. Under the banner of "Protect Water, Protect Life" they marched south from the respective coasts and along the way groups mapped a total of 500 major polluting units, various illegal encroachments by industrial units, numerous commercial aquaculture projects, and displacement of coastal villages. In addition, they demanded the closure of the nuclear power plant to be built in Kanyakumari (at the southern tip of India where waters of the Bay of Bengal and the Arabian Sea merge) where the *yatra* ended. This *yatra* set into motion struggles across the country against what NFF has termed the "looting of the coast." In response to these struggles, the government of India enacted the Coastal Regulation Zone (CRZ) Notification in 1991 to "establish a statutory and administrative mechanism to control destructive development activities on the coast."

Yet, CRZ has the dubious distinction of being one of the most violated notifications. The government itself has amended it twenty-five times to open the coast to industrial development in violation of its intent, and in 2008 the government sought to formalize this by changing the notification from Coastal Regulation Zone to Coastal Management Zone. It was to oppose this change that in 2008 the NFF organized a *Machimar Adhikhar Rashtriya Abhiyan* (National Campaign for Fishers' Rights) led by its then-chairperson Harekrishan Debnath that brought him to Kutch and to BSetu. The campaign traveled the entire 7000-km coastline of India and held meetings in fishing villages and hamlets to raise awareness of the change in the CRZ notification and to mobilize fishers against it. The campaign ended in New Delhi with a huge rally of thousands of fishers from all across the country. Thirty fishers from Mundra attended this rally at their own cost. As Ibrahimkaka said of this rally:

> I had heard that as I am a citizen the *sarkar*, government, has to help us whenever there is trouble. I wanted to see where the sarkar is. First, we went to Gandhinagar looking for it. But then we heard that there is an even bigger animal that resides in Delhi, so we went there and I stood there and called out to our big chief. We met with the PM, there were fisherfolks from 9 states and we told him to send a ruling in our favor.
> (Interview February 17, 2011).

In response to this large mobilization, the government withdrew its proposed changes and initiated consultations with fishing communities in all the states, resulting in a revised CRZ in 2011, which includes a role for fishers in developing a coastal zone management plan (CZMP), as well as a district-level coastal committee, which allows fishers to work with the state in regulating the development of the coast. As Menon and Kohli (2013) note, while the CZMP is mostly vague, the district-level committees are a tool that fishers and their organizations can use, but to date no state has yet established such committees.

Thus, MASS emerged as part of a national mobilization against a policy change. MASS has members not only from Kutch, but also from Saurashtra and mainland Gujarat. The membership of Kutch MASS is around 650, with another 350 members in Saurashtra. Bhadreshwar has the largest and most active MASS, with around 250 members. This has meant that since 2009 when the public hearing for the OPG power plant was held in Bhadreshwar, the focus of MASS has primarily been to prevent the construction of the power plant in Bhadreshwar. Although MASS has equal representation of men and women in its membership and leadership (e.g., the vice-president of MASS is a woman), it is mostly inactive. There are no formal meetings or elections, and the elder men of the community from Bhadreshwar make most of the decisions about the struggle through informal discussions with each other and BSetu staff.

Like the Gram Swaraj Samiti mentioned in the context of the Mahuva movement, MASS is invoked and mobilized when necessary. So unlike poor people's movement organizations that become formalized and lose their radical edge (e.g., Piven and Cloward, 1978), MASS, like the other two struggles highlighted in the book, is an example of an informal movement structure that remains latent until needed and hence does not need resources for maintenance otherwise. Such an informal structure is anchored, however, by organizations with more formal structures such as Abhiyan and BSetu, which continue to ensure the participation of fisher women in the major protest activities, such as public hearings and meetings with state officials and expert committees that have come to Bhadreshwar in response to the legal challenges mounted by MASS against the OPG power plant.

Legalism from below in the struggle and beyond

The fishers in Bhadreshwar began hearing rumors about the construction of a power plant in their village around the time they formed MASS in 2008. As Ibrahimkaka said, "[J]ust as crows caw and we know that something is happening we heard rumors from people and knew we had to get ready" (Interview February 17, 2011). The rumors were confirmed when the public hearing of the OPG power plant was announced. It was held on May 29, 2009, in Bhadreshwar village at Chokhanda *mandir*, a local temple. The Gujarat Pollution Control Board Regional Officer, Mr. Kalyani, and Kutch Additional Collector Mr. Vaghela chaired the meeting. OPG project director Mr. Padmanabhan, along with other company officials, were present, as were officers from Detox Corporation, a Surat-based agency that carried out the Environment Impact Assessment (EIA) and wrote the report. Over 200 people from the surrounding villages marched in a rally that ended at the public hearing site. There were fishers, saltpan workers, pastoralists, farmers, and villagers from Bhadreshwar and the surrounding villages of Sangad, Wandi, Luni, Hatdi, and Pavdiara. MASS, which had been formed a year earlier, and BSetu were instrumental in this mobilization. The *gram panchayats* of eleven affected villages submitted letters opposing the OPG project at the public hearing. Although the meeting was held on Friday, the

Muslim Sabbath, the fishers all came to the hearing chanting, "We will give our life but not our livelihood" (from the MASS website, http://masskutch.blogspot.com/, accessed June 5, 2013).

The public hearings are both highly scripted and spontaneous events. MASS members, along with BSetu, Abhiyan staff, and activists of various local NGOs and advocacy groups such as *Lok Adhikar Manch* (People's Rights Forum) and regional NGOs such as *Paryavaran Mitra* that were active in the Mahuva movement as well, had worked for weeks to prepare critiques of the EIA and the EMP (Environment Management Plan) and articulate the communities' demands. Community members were trained to testify, and care was taken to be inclusive. For example, among the speakers were Soniben from *Lok Adhikar Manch* and a *dalit* leader, Valjibhai, in addition to several fishers and saltpan workers. Soniben highlighted the plight of widows in the area who had for many years been demanding five acres of land for every widow. She noted that while the collector refused to even meet with them, he eagerly met with industry leaders and readily signed away land.

Grievance narratives (e.g., Davis, 2002; Polletta, 1998) are carefully constructed and located historically as well as within the state's rhetoric of social justice, citizenship, and environmental sustainability As movement scholars have noted, how issues are framed and how they resonate within the community as well as with the authorities is crucial to the success of protest narratives (e.g., Benford and Snow, 2000). In its grievance narrative, MASS highlighted two ways in which the plant would affect local communities, their livelihood, and their environment.

First, MASS challenged the OPG claim that there is no substantial commercial fishing in the area. They noted that small-scale artisanal fisheries, like the local *pagadiyas*, constitute 40% of fishing in India and over 2,000 local villagers have been fishing here for two centuries, moving to the *bandars* during the fishing season and in the off-season back to their homes in the villages. Because of this movement back and forth, fishers have been unable to gain ownership of the coastal land, which makes their situation precarious despite their long history in the area. Similarly, 5,000 acres of saltpans, which provide livelihood to hundreds of saltpan workers, were not listed by the EIA. After establishing the existence of various livelihoods in the region, they demonstrated how the 540 lakh liters of water that would be taken in and 360 lakh liters that would be discharged into the sea by the power plant would result in an end to fishing due to changes in salinity and water temperatures.

Second, the protestors demonstrated the ways in which the power plant would affect their environment. From the increasing pollution due to the ash and toxic gases that would be generated by the power plant to the daily traffic and pollution from the 150 to 200 trucks that would be required to bring the coal from the port in Mundra, 30 km away, their fragile ecosystem, protected by the CRZ, would be significantly altered. As noted earlier, their coastline is an intertidal zone of the Gulf of Kutch, rich in biodiversity, from mangroves to mudflats and coral reefs to rare species of fish and other fauna. Finally, the protestors highlighted the fact that 316 acres of ecologically sensitive coastal land, sold at great subsidy and in violation of the CRZ, would be supplying power to the industries along the coast but not to the local people. Given all these concerns, they asked: "Why not locate the plant in a less ecologically sensitive site?" *Dalit* leader Valjibhai even proposed an alternative site in the Little Rann, the smaller of the two deserts in Kutch. Thus, preparing for public hearings and participating in them are important mechanisms of legalism from below. They enable subaltern groups not only to understand how the law can be used to challenge their dispossession, but also to think more broadly about law as an "expression of the will of the community."

Following the public hearing, without waiting for environmental clearance, OPG organized a *bhoomi puja*, a groundbreaking ceremony, and began construction. This led to protest by 7,000 people, some of whom broke the fences of the power plant, which resulted in the arrests of thirty fishers. Upon their release, one of the leaders was co-opted by the company, but the majority of them were ready to continue the struggle. On August 9, 2009, with the guidance of Anandbhai Yagnik, also the lawyer for the Mahuva movement, MASS filed a Public Interest Litigation (PIL) in the Gujarat High Court.

The Gujarat High Court sent an expert committee to study the site and the claims of the litigants and in February 2010 ruled that OPG could not proceed with construction unless it obtained the requisite environmental clearance. OPG managed to get this certificate in June 2010 by withholding key information. Still, in response to the protests and the PIL, the State Environment Impact Appraisal Authority imposed 121 conditions that OPG had to address to protect the interests of the fishers, saltpan workers, and other affected villagers. Among the conditions were to change the technology of the power plant from a water-cooled system to an air-cooled one. OPG restarted work without meeting all those conditions, leading to a show cause notice from the State Board of Pollution.

At the same time, Bharatbhai, on the advice of advocates, began to document the unlawful construction at the site using Google Earth images and photographs to document the violation of the Gujarat Pollution Board's recommendations. In response, the state-level expert appraisal committee sought an explanation from OPG. Instead of responding to the committee, OPG rolled out a corporate social responsibility (CSR) plan, which outlined how they would employ local villagers and set aside monies for social development. MASS rejected the plan and sent a memo to the national Ministry of Environment and Forests (MoEF) asking for a meeting. Several MASS members and Bharatbhai met with the minister of MoEF, Mr. Jayaram Ramesh, on November 30, 2010. The minister promised to send an investigative committee, which finally arrived on February 14, 2012. Based on the committee's report, the National Green Tribunal directed OPG to desist further construction until all approvals were obtained. In gross violation of these legal orders, OPG continued construction, resulting in the near-complete structure that I saw in November 2013.

When MASS filed another petition with the National Green Tribunal they were fined Rs. 10,000 for wasting the tribunal's time through excessive complaints. In response MASS filed a review petition, and the date to hear that petition was set for late November 2013. As of this writing, MASS has yet to hear from the Green Tribunal. So the struggle continues in the legal arena.

But legalism from below goes beyond using the law to make the state accountable. It also involves engaging subaltern women and men in a critical and collective democratic process. MASS members have been doing so in a couple of ways, as I discuss next.

Rights-based planning in gram panchayats

During my stay in Kutch in 2011, Sushmaben conducted a week-long training on a rights-based approach to planning for elected *sarpanchs*. Various policy makers and activists from across the state were brought in, including a Skype session with an activist in Pune, to explain various aspects of a rights-based approach to planning and to engage *sarpanchs* in designing a plan for their respective villages.

The training included three different kinds of sessions: (1) theoretical ones that highlighted concepts of democracy; rights; relationships among various levels of governance; and principles of justice, equity, and active citizenship and how they as *sarpanchs* fit into this terrain; (2) substantive ones that focused on the current model of development, who bore the costs versus who enjoyed the benefits, current understandings about land and water use, crop diversity and local varieties, animal husbandry and other Kutch-specific social and economic issues; and (3) more hands-on sessions where the participants mapped out issues and plans for their specific villages in dialogue with the other leaders. Each *sarpanch* was given a laptop, and computer literacy was also an important part of the training.

In the theoretical sessions, among the issues discussed were citizenship versus leadership, the different kinds of rights, and principles of planning.

The majority of the sessions were substantive and focused on how land and water are the villages' principle assets over which the villagers have control and a right to plan in keeping with their interests. For example, one of the speakers noted that unlike other parts of India, in Kutch almost 75% of land was still held in common and should be saved that way. Similarly, it was important to use water in sustainable ways through check dams and harvesting rainwater rather than digging deeper and deeper into the aquifers, undermining the water table for future generations.

There were sessions on maintaining diversity of food crops and understanding the true costs of industrial agriculture. The focus was on the need to grow staples such as *bajra*, millet, and legumes, rather than the current focus on cash crops such as cumin, castor oil, cotton, and fruits. An interesting point the speaker made in this regard was if you do not know where your produce goes then you should not grow it on more than 10% of your land. He made similar comments about fruit orchards, which are water intensive and the products cannot be stored for as long as food grains. Other sessions highlighted the need to think not only of humans but also other living beings as having a right to land and water, thus maintaining *gauchar*, or commons, for pasture. Such training enables subaltern women and men to become better informed and be better leaders.

Beyond such training for democratic governance, MASS members were also involved in articulating legal mechanisms for a more inclusive development.

Ground-truthing for an alternative development

In February 2012 MASS joined with other villagers, Ujjas and BSetu staff, activists, journalists, and other concerned citizens in Mundra *taluka* to form an informal collective called the *Mundra Hit Rakshak Manch* (Forum for Protection of Rights in Mundra). The forum emerged organically from a year-long community-led effort of "ground-truthing"[11] to document the impact of the proposed waterfront development, one of the largest infrastructure and industrial projects in Mundra, to be undertaken by Adani Corporation. The community-led exercise included pastoralists, horticulturalists, and farmers who were also concerned with the development of this project. The ground-truthing exercise involved villagers as knowledge producers and as learners. As knowledge producers, they gathered evidence about the local impact of this project that included narratives, documents, photos, and petitions. They also learned about the necessary environmental clearances required for such projects and the ways in which the Gujarat Pollution Control Board was in violation of national notifications.

They met at various points to discuss whether their strategy should be to oppose industrialization or to focus on policy and regulatory mechanisms. They recognized that given the rapid industrialization that had already taken place over the past two decades, the best they could hope for was ensuring the sustainability of their livelihoods and protecting the coast that remained free from industrialization. All the evidence gathered was shared with the expert committee sent by the national Ministry of Environment and Forests to evaluate the impact of the waterfront development. The Adani Corporation had received environmental clearance for this project in 2009 along with seventeen specific and fourteen general mandatory conditions (Mundra Hit Rakshak Manch et al, 2013). The conditions related to preventing the destruction of mangroves; blocking of creeks or fishers' vessels; and not disturbing the sand dunes, coral reefs, and mudflats in the area. Yet, by 2012 the Manch found that Adani had not fulfilled the reporting obligations and despite the show cause notice issued by the MoEF had continued building.

Hence, along with *Kheti Vikas Sewa* Trust (Trust for Agricultural Development and Welfare), MASS petitioned the Ministry of Environment and Forests in New Delhi to establish a committee to assess the impact of the Adani Port, Thermal Power Plant, and Special Economic Zone on environmental safety and integrity in Mundra. The ministry appointed a five-member committee of experts in September 2012. The committee conducted a site visit in January 2013 during which they met with members of MASS and BSetu staff who showed them around the *bandars* and the creeks to demonstrate the violations and the impact on their livelihoods. Though the livelihood of fishers was not part of the committee's charge, given MASS's input the committee added a section on it and the ways in which they have been affected.

Specifically, the expert committee noted the impeded access of fishers to their fishing grounds, the unimplemented promises to build infrastructure and fishing harbors, the depletion of fish in the area, and the poor living conditions of the community:

> The development on the coast – which was inhabited by them – had clearly little space for them. It is clear that this community, which depends on the coasts for their livelihood is the most vulnerable and most hit by development projects. Their economy depends on the health of the sea and its interface with land. Projects at the coast do not often respect the rights of fisherfolk, as unlike farmers and settled villagers, their access is not encoded and recognized. This is what clearly has happened in Mundra and needs to be urgently addressed.
> (Expert Committee of the Ministry of Environment and Forests Report, 2013: 68)

It then goes on to recommend that there must be a specific plan for each community to ensure their livelihood and welfare and such a plan should be more than just commitments on paper. Its overall observation was that there were massive ecological changes that adversely affected the communities who lived along the coast. The committee found many lapses and violations, including the lack of mandatory public hearings, the requisite environmental clearances, the blockage of creeks, cutting of mangroves, and pollution.

The committee observed that initiating legal proceedings for non-compliance would only take time and not guarantee any concrete remedies. So it made concrete recommendations, such as cancellation of the North Port that had not yet been constructed, building a fishing harbor within two years exclusively for fishers in Bhadreshwar; and the creation of an environmental restoration fund of 1% of the project cost for remedial action to restore creeks and plant mangroves. Ultimately, their recommendation was for a strong deterrent, restoration, and, most importantly, for a strong regulatory and policy system of coastal zone management so there would be monitoring in the public domain, which would ensure that such committees would not be necessary in the future.

Along with seeking such policy changes, Bharatbhai (at the time of this writing) is working more specifically with the Center for Policy Research's Environment Justice Program to develop a proposal that would declare the stretch of the coast with the seven *bandars* an ecologically sensitive zone that will restrict development to that which is ecologically sustainable and guarantee coastal rights to those who have been fishing here for generations. Fishers on each *bandar* discussed this proposal and supported it as the best way to ensure their livelihood and protect their waters. Bharatbhai and others are in conversation with the Gujarat State Pollution Board and the national MoEF about the feasibility of such a proposal.

The active participation of subaltern women in these processes is a result of the ongoing work of BSetu and MASS with women's movement organizations in the local field of protest.

Towards a gender-just geography of struggle

Ujjas (Light) *Mahila Sangathan* (Women's Organization, hence forth Ujjas), located in Mundra town about 30 km from Bhadreshwar, is the key women's movement organization that works with BSetu and MASS on an ongoing basis around issues of gender justice. Ujjas works with fisher and *rabari* women around economic and political empowerment. Ujjas was started by Kutch Mahilla Vikas Sangathan (Kutch Women's Development Organization, henceforth KMVS) in 1991 to work with poor rural women.

KMVS itself was founded by Sushma Ayengar, along with others, in 1989 to empower rural women through collectives (see www.kmvs.org.in). KMVS was among the groups that emerged in the context of the autonomous women's movement in the country. Its founder member, Sushma Ayengar, was committed to working with rural women and came to Kutch in response to opportunities provided by a state bureaucrat and the women's collective that she was a part of in Ahmedabad.

Following her work with Muslim women in the Banni region of Kutch, she worked with local women to start KMVS, whose goals were to organize poor women around livelihood issues and gender equality. One of the ways they did this was through the formation of cooperatives to enhance the work that poor women did throughout the region. For example, various communities in Kutch have rich traditions of embroidery with each one noted for a particular type of work. Hence, the first cooperatives were for embroidery production. The cooperatives could sell their products directly to customers through KMVS stores and outlets.

KMVS defines itself as a movement to empower women to become decision makers. As such, in the words of its founder, there were some non-negotiables. Among them was not to be a service provider or implementer of government projects and programs. Their focus is to organize women and then enable them to mobilize resources from multiple sources. Process is as important for the staff of KMVS as it is for the women's collectives they organize. Thus, self-reflection and critique and term limits for leaders are built into its work. This has resulted in KMVS being led by its third generation of leaders. Most activists have a very clear sense of their methodology and strategy of organizing and networking, even with government when necessary, and then moving on to a new phase of work. "This deep thinking about process, developing expertise and decentralizing, and methodology of not implementing but building capacity of local women, mostly in the rural areas first and now in the urban areas is what explains our success" (Interview with Sushma Ayengar February 12, 2011).

From one collective of rural women, KMVS is now a network of seven grassroots women's organizations, Ujjas being one of them, working with around 20,000 women across Kutch. Ujjas began work in eight villages around women's empowerment and now works in forty-six villages with around 4,500 rural women, including the fishers from the seven *bandars*. Given that BSetu, Abhiyan, KMVS, and Ujjas are all part of the same nested structure, the basic philosophy and methodology of work with the rural poor is the same: the economic, social, and political empowerment of rural poor through self-governing collectives. Ujjas is run by a board, which is composed entirely of poor women who make all the decisions about the direction of the organization. The staff of Ujjas focuses on capacity building of poor women around economic and political issues.

Ujjas began by organizing poor women in self-help groups (SHGs) for consciousness raising and livelihood collectives. The SHG for the fisher women focused on establishing savings and training them to become more active in the producer company. Ujjas is currently working to establish a women's bank following the model of SEWA in Ahmedabad. Along with the Kutch Sea Food Company and BSetu, Ujjas also organizes training for fisher women to upgrade their skills for sorting and drying fish and takes them on "exposure" visits to other fisher collectives in Gujarat. As a result, many fisher women have become active in Ujjas and the current chair of Ujjas' board is a fisher woman. Such engagement with Ujjas has also increased the fisher women's mobility. Although they work on the coast, most women seldom leave their villages. Now, however, they routinely travel to the Ujjas office or state administrative offices in Mundra, 10 to 30 km away from their home villages.

In response to women's concerns about violence against women, Ujjas has begun to offer counseling and other services for women experiencing violence (Interview with Reenaben February 8, 2011). When the 1993 Panchayati Raj Act went into effect, Ujjas began training women for participation in *panchayat* elections. Their *panchayat* training has resulted in many women running for election, and in Bhadreshwar, Aminamasi, a respected elder in the fisher community, served as *sarpanch*. Since the formation of MASS and the start of protests against OPG, Ujjas has worked to ensure the representation of women and their perspective in MASS and the struggle.

What neither BSetu, Ujjas, nor Abhiyan can alter is the gender segregation of social and political spaces in the village, such as the BSetu office, which is the nerve center of the struggle, the newly built *gram panchayat* space, or the tea shops on the highway where men gather most days and where informal conversations take place. The BSetu office has for the most part been an exclusively male space. The office is in a small compound composed of five buildings, two of which serve as residential spaces for the staff, one is a training/seminar space, one an office, and the last a kitchen.[12] The two residential spaces were built to provide space for men and women staff, but they have not been able to recruit any women staff. Given the hardships of rural life, including its gender segregation, living in a mixed-gender residential space is not easy for either subaltern or middle-class women. During my first research season, one of the two research fellows at BSetu was a young fisher woman with a social work background. At the end of her fellowship, she returned to her town on the island of Diu.

Thus, given the strong commitment to gender justice within the local field of protest in Kutch, subaltern women in MASS are more consistently involved in the struggle. But the changing dynamics within the struggle demonstrate other gender fault lines.

The changing dynamics within the struggle

Six years after the public hearing and even as the power plant nears completion, MASS activists are still fiery and committed to stopping the completion of the power plant. When I mentioned to several activists that the power plant was scheduled to begin generating power in March 2014, one of the activists, and now a deputy *sarpanch* of the village *panchayat* said, "That may be so but we will not let it happen," cryptically adding, "We will take one last shot to ensure that it does not begin." As of this writing, the plant is not yet functional.

Most MASS activists and even BSetu staff see the struggle as 80% successful, as they were able to get the plant to change its technology from a low-cost water-cooled system to a more expensive but less damaging air-cooled system. It is the only instance in India where a subaltern struggle has led to such technological changes in the design of a power plant. But the fishers are not satisfied with this and seek the dismantling of the plant altogether.

The non-fisher staff of BSetu do not see the dismantling of the plant as very likely. Given the importance of electricity to the economic growth of the country, a power plant is seen differently than a cement factory, even by the Congress party, the party the fishers support. Now with BJP rule at the national level, it is less likely that the fisher struggle will get a sympathetic hearing. Despite the political factors against the struggle, most BSetu activists are skeptical that the plant will become operational any time soon, given the delays and changes in the energy sector, which will affect its profitability.

What they are concerned about, however, are the response of MASS leaders to the Corporate Social Responsibility (CSR) initiatives of OPG and other corporations, especially Adani, the main corporate actor in the area. By law, corporations now have to invest 2% of their net profits in CSR. There is a clear division between the fishers, primarily male leaders, and non-fisher activists on this. For the fishers, accepting any CSR monies is tantamount to betrayal and a death knell of their livelihoods. At the same time, they are not against development per se. As Ibrahimkaka's poem with which I began the chapter illustrates, they would welcome non-polluting factories that produce goods for the consumption of local people. They oppose destructive industries that do not benefit the local communities. The non-fishers agree with them about the need for environmentally friendly industries to benefit the local communities, but also want to work constructively with the existing industries.

This dilemma is best exemplified by the construction of the private school by the Adani Foundation. As noted earlier, the current facilities for education on the coast are non-existent to inadequate, despite the efforts of local NGOs and individual patrons. The Adani Foundation built a school in Bhadreshwar specifically for the fishers' children. The community, however, sees this as an effort to co-opt them and assure their cooperation with Adani's future waterfront development plans, so they do not send their children to the school. Only five fisher kids are in the school and the rest of the school is filled with children from other communities in Bhadreshwar and surrounding villages – this, despite the efforts of the *gram panchayat* to include a clause in the school's charter that would guarantee free education for the fisher children in perpetuity. The fishers saw the *panchayat*'s action as betrayal. Although this position reflects a large majority of the fishers, there are some in the community, especially women, who are more ambivalent, especially as there is great competition in the other communities to send their children to this school with excellent teachers and facilities. The BSetu staff understands the fishers' position, but are concerned that in the meantime their children are not receiving an education.

Similar polarization has occurred around the *panchayat*'s use of CSR monies for the development of basic services such as water pipelines in the community and to their temporary homes on the coast. The elected *sarpanch* of the village is a woman from the *darbar* community. MASS agreed to her candidacy, as they recognized that a fisher woman would not have received the support of the entire village. But the de facto *sarpanch* of the village is her brother-in-law who makes all the decisions, calls the meetings, and even receives all the official mail. The *sarpanch* seldom leaves her house or engages in the business of the village. Six of the nine members of the *panchayat* are fishers and MASS members. The brother-in-law supports the MASS protests against the OPG power plant, but he does not think that precludes using CSR monies from other corporations such as Tata and Adani. The MASS members of the *panchayat* do not agree with him and feel betrayed. The BSetu staff is in agreement with the de facto *sarpanch*'s pragmatic approach, but is reluctant to force the issue with the fishers.

The BSetu staff is concerned with this all-or-nothing position of MASS, as it prevents them from thinking about their long-term issues of sustainability. Most BSetu staff members are afraid to push this issue with MASS, as they do not want to be seen as co-opted by corporate interests. Both Bharatbhai and Usmanbhai felt that the new CEO of the Adani Foundation, responsible for its CSR initiatives, is interested in working with the fishers. But MASS members will not even entertain the idea, as they consider it selling out. Hence, BSetu staff members also do not engage the foundation.[13]

The new CEO of Adani Foundation, Mr. Saxena, has changed many of the corporation's earlier positions regarding their impact on the fishers' livelihood and the environment. For example, from refusing to acknowledge the destruction of the mangroves, the foundation now acknowledges their loss and the need to protect the fishers' livelihood and their long-term sustainability. Towards that end, they have provided more permanent shelters with toilets and water and solar electricity on Junna *bandar* close to the Adani port. Mr. Saxena claims that they would like to extend those benefits to all the *bandars* but MASS members prevent them from doing so. That is not completely accurate, as not all MASS members on all the *bandars* are opposed to such facilities. As Usmanbhai notes, while the Adani Foundation's thinking may be undergoing some change, their strategies of working with the people remain the same.

When I met with Mr. Saxena, he acknowledged that Adani Corporation had erred in the past in the way they approached the fishing community by working with a leader who did not really represent the people, so understandably, the fishers mistrust the foundation. Consequently, it will take time to "break the ice," as he put it, but he intends to keep trying to work with the community and with other actors, including the state, to work not just on immediate issues facing the community, but also for their long-term sustainability. He then went on to outline his multi-pronged approach, beginning with securing land titles on the coast to ensure that fishers have rights to state services; building basic facilities on each *bandar* such as water, electricity, school, health care clinics and roads; livelihood opportunities during the period when they are in their villages and not fishing; and more options for the younger generation who might desire other livelihoods. He also mentioned the need to develop marine industries like artificial coral reefs for pearls and aquaculture for export.

When I asked him what was preventing him from implementing such a plan, he said he was trying to build a relationship with the fishers and also get support from the fisheries commissioner who he acknowledged is so opposed to fishing as an occupation, based on his own vegetarianism, that it has been a challenge to make progress. Ghassem-Fachandi's (2011) work confirms how BJP makes political use of vegetarianism by promoting "the visceral disgust" that many upper-caste Gujaratis feel for meat eaters, the code word for Muslims, though most *dalits* and other lower castes also eat meat. I heard this in reference to the fishers many times during my stay in Gujarat. Most of what Mr. Saxena outlined are demands that fishers have been making for decades. And as the fishers and BSetu staff noted when I told them about his plan, that is all well and good, but when is he going to meet with them and ask them what they think.

This back and forth between the fishers and corporations and the differences between the BSetu staff and MASS male members demonstrate the dilemmas in subaltern struggles that go beyond the immediate aim of the protests to the long-term sustainability of the community. MASS has tried to address some of these issues with their multi-pronged approach and their work with multiple local, regional, and national actors.

Conclusion

What is distinctive about MASS is the ways in which it evolved out of ongoing work by a community-based organization with a particular vision and methodology, which in turn was embedded in a larger network of NGOs that had transformed from providing relief and rehabilitation during natural disasters to one oriented to social change. Although many aspects of MASS are unique to Kutch and its particular history and geography, there are others that provide important insights for social justice in general and gender justice in particular. I highlight some of those insights here, but return to them in the concluding chapter of the book.

Abhiyan, the network of NGOs, and the transformation in its goals provide keys to possibilities for how poor communities can be engaged in and shape their own possibilities. The network itself was a response to recurrent natural disasters. Such crises enabled organizations that do not share a philosophy of social change to come together. But while they may have not shared a philosophy and methodology of work, all the organizations in the network were part of what Levi and Olson (2000) have called a community of fate. Within such a community, organizations recognize common goals with each other and the need for solidarity against common enemies. This shared commitment allowed differently positioned actors to engage each other constructively and be open to the others in the network. This trust, along with the leadership of key activists and their normative commitments (Ahlquist and Levi, 2013), facilitated the shift in the goal of the network from a short-term, crisis-oriented response to a longer-term strategy of empowering communities to work for social justice.

Setus highlight the ways in which the organizing traditions of the key leaders in the network were translated via explicit goals and methodology into bridge organizations working in the communities. Focusing on collective rather than individual solutions based on self-governance and through capacity building laid a solid foundation for social justice work. Targeting women further ensured that gender justice would be an integral part of social justice. Delineating three realms – livelihood, information exchange, and decentralized planning – enabled self-reliance and good governance based on informed citizenship. Hiring and training staff through workshops and collective dialogues ensured that such commitments were translated into the work done in communities. Thus, structured mechanisms such as ongoing training, dialogue, "ground-truthing," and cooperatives were key to democratic praxis and facilitating the active citizenship of subaltern women and men.

It was this political praxis that resulted in Bharatbhai's working with fishers in Bhadreshwar and building the producer company as well as the *bandar panchayats*. Being connected with fishers' struggles across the country facilitated the formation of MASS and created an organizational structure for protest. Thus, while the terrain of struggle is local, the solidarities are translocal and national. Although registered as a union, MASS is informally organized and is invoked only when necessary. While this reduces organizational costs for poor people's organizations, it also means that an informal leadership of elder men makes most of the decisions. But by forming ongoing relationships with women's movement organizations such as Ujjas, women's political agency is also assured. Thus, the relationship with women's movement organizations, along with the ideology and praxis of its movement anchor, BSetu, led to sustained gender justice work even among communities that continue to retain gender segregation in public spaces and a gendered division of labor. Such realities on the ground alert us to rethinking assumptions about gendered division of labor and its relationship to gender justice. They might not necessarily be contradictory, provided there are structured mechanisms to ensure women's participation, leadership, and empowerment as economic and political actors.

The differences between fishers and BSetu staff and local elected officials reveal tensions that are not easy to resolve and that have consequences for the material lives of fishers. I turn to these and other theoretical and practical issues raised by all three struggles in the next and concluding chapter.

Notes

1 A Sanskrit word denoting God.
2 Ibrahimkaka shared this poem with me.
3 Bhadreshwar village is 5 kms from *Randh bandar* (harbor or fishing pier), where fishing will be most affected by the OPG power plant. Fishers from many villages fish *at Randh bandar* but a majority of them come from Bhadreshwar.
4 In Kutch, staff members and activists were very sensitive to the issue of naming. Most activists and staff saw themselves as part of a movement rather than an NGO. According to them, the most important distinction between the two is that an NGO uses donor funds to provide services, while a movement organizes the local community and empowers them to be self-governing. By that definition, Setus are hybrids, though to outsiders they are NGOs, as they do not provide services but organize the local communities; but they also have paid staff, who are funded by various donors via its parent body, Abhiyan.
5 The earthquake was felt in twenty-one of the twenty-five districts of Gujarat. In Kutch, over 12,000 lives were lost, and over 14,000 were severely injured, while in Gujarat as a whole, over 100,000 lives were lost.

6 The Setus were funded by the Swiss Agency for Development and Cooperation, United Nations Development Programme, and National Tree Growers' Cooperative Federation. Their rehabilitation efforts after the earthquake in 2001 were so successful that since then they have provided guidance to other rehabilitation efforts. For example, after the 2004 tsunami in Indonesia, in Jammu and Kashmir following their earthquake in 2005, and in Bihar following the 2008 floods.
7 Cooperatives have a special history in Gujarat, which is home to one of the most successful dairy cooperatives in the country. Kaira District Milk Producers Union, popularly called AMUL, was launched in 1948 and has grown from two village milk-producing societies to 378 village societies and has 68,000 members (www.amuldairy.com). In addition to AMUL, Gujarat is home to SEWA, the Self-Employed Women's Association, which unionized informal-sector workers and then organized production cooperatives beginning in 1972 for urban and rural women.
8 Abhiyan has partnered with many training institutions throughout Gujarat through its Abhiyan College of Para Professional Education for Rural Youth to provide such training. To date, they have trained 300 youths.
9 Bharatbhai holds a master's degree in rural management from Gujarat Vidyapeeth, the Gandhian University in Ahmedabad, and is the first in his rural family to have a college degree. His alma mater gave him their highest alumni award in 2012 in recognition of his decade-long work with the fishers in Kutch.
10 The largest being the Sunderbans in West Bengal.
11 Ground-truthing is an epistemology and a methodology of knowing the realities on the ground from those living them and through their participation.
12 All the eighteen Setus share a similar design and configuration of buildings.
13 On the day that one of the BSetu staff members took me to meet the CEO of the Adani Foundation, he invented a lie to avoid being seen with the foundation staff, as that would undermine his credibility in the community.

References

Ahlquist, John and Margaret Levi. 2013. *In the Interest of Others: Organizations and Social Activism*. Princeton: Princeton University Press.

Benford, Robert, and David Snow. 2000. "Framing Processes and Social Movements: An Overview." *Annual Review of Sociology* 26:611–639.

Bhandari, Vivek. 2010. "Organizational Forms in Flux: Cooperative and Producer Companies." Anand: Institute of Rural Management Anand.

Davis, Joseph, editor. 2002. *Stories of Change: Narratives and Social Movements*. Albany: State University of New York Press.

Expert Committee of the Ministry of Environment and Forests. 2013. *Report of the Committee for Inspection of M/s Adani Port & SEZ LTD. Mundra, Gujarat*. New Delhi: Ministry of Environment and Forests.

Ghassem-Fachandi, Parvis. 2011. "On the political use of disgust in Gujarat." In *Gujarat Beyond Gandhi: Identity, Society, and Conflict*, 91–110. Edited by Nalin Mehta and Mona Mehta. London: Routledge.

Levi, Margaret and David Olson. 2000. 'The Battles in Seattle." *Politics & Society* 28(3):217–37.

Menon, Manju and Kanchi Kohli. 2013. "Keep the Coasts Clear for Small-Scale Fishermen." Report on the website of Namati-CPR Environment Justice Program.

Mundra Hit Rakshak Manch, Machimar Adhikar Sangharsh Sangathan, Ujjas Mahila Sangathan, and *Namati*-Centre for Policy Research Environment Justice Program. 2013. *Closing The Enforcement Gap: Findings of A Community Led Ground Truthing of Environmental Violations in Mundra, Kutch.* New Delhi: Namati-CPR Environment Justice Program.

Piven, Francis Fox and Richard Cloward. 1978. *Poor People's Movements: Why They Succeed How They Fail.* New York: Vintage.

Polletta, Francesca. 1998. "Contending Stories: Narratives in Social Movements." *Qualitative Sociology* 21(4):419–446.

Setu. n.d. *Setu Bhuj: Kutch Nav Nirman Abhiyan.*

Sheth, D. L. 2007. "Micro-movements in India: Towards a New Politics of Participatory Democracy." In *Democratizing Democracy: Beyond the Liberal Democratic Canon*, 3–37. Edited by Boaventura De Sousa Santos. London: Verso.

6 Towards a gender-just development and democracy

On May 16, 2014, Narendra Modi and the Bharatiya Janata Party (BJP) won a resounding mandate in the national elections, winning 275 out of 543 seats. It was the first time since 1989 that any single party had won such a majority. Many supporters joyously shouted, "The nation has been "*Modi*-fied," against the term's usage as a critical expression in Gujarat meant to challenge his authoritarian politics. One of the main reasons cited by pundits and some scholars alike for his victory was the "Gujarat model" of development. Voters, they argued, tired with the dysfunctions of Congress's coalition politics, the uneven gains from economic growth resulting in continuing poverty, and the rampant corruption, sought change. Modi, with his reputation for corruption-free good governance and creating a vibrant Gujarat, was just what the frustrated voters desired. This even trumped the taint on his administration of the deaths of over a thousand Muslims in 2002 on his watch and under his authoritarian Hindutva politics.

But as the three struggles in this book demonstrate, this narrative of the Gujarat model that Modi successfully sold to the nation is a partial one. Although Gujarat certainly is business friendly,[1] has undergone rapid industrialization, and has improved its infrastructure, many of the foundations for such advances were laid before Modi, and their benefits have gone disproportionately to the elite and middle classes at the expense of the poor. In Ahmedabad, the polarity between the Hindu and Muslim neighborhoods is particularly stark. Moreover, as Jeffrey (2014) notes, what most supporters of Modi and the Gujarat model failed to note is "that among India's states Gujarat ranks around the midway point on most indicators of human development, such as primary school education, female literacy and child nutrition."

Moreover, as I have shown in the foregoing chapters, the grievances of the struggles were also the result of Modi's Gujarat model. In the case of the Sangathan, the seven dams that are to be constructed in the *adivasi* villages as part of the Par-Tapi Link Project were initially conceived in the 1950s during the heyday of state developmentalism, when large dams were deemed temples of development. However, it was not until the successful completion of the Narmada dam in 2005, under Modi, that the project gained momentum. Similarly, the construction of the cement factory in the midst of agriculturally productive land and a power plant along the coast where fishers earned their livelihoods in a protected coastal zone were a result of his business-friendly land policies. These policies made it possible for the state to sanction land to private corporations at minimal cost and to undermine environmental regulations in the name of development.

But what the struggles in the book also show is that in spite of these policies and the dominant climate of privatization, there are also possibilities for subaltern groups to challenge them, and sometimes to succeed, offering insights for a gender-just development and democracy for subaltern groups.

Challenging development in Gujarat: legalism from below, translocal fields of protest, and gendered geographies

All three struggles emerged in response to the subaltern groups' dispossession from their land and livelihood. Although only the Sangathan struggle was against a state-led project, as the Mahuva cement factory and the OPG power plant were private development projects, all three struggles challenged the state. This targeting of the state by the three struggles, and hundreds of others underway in India, as Levien (2013) argues, is a consequence of the state's important role as a land broker and its justifications for dispossessing people from their land. Part of the repertoire of all three struggles against the state was legalism from below, made possible, in part, by the changing legal architecture of the state.

The Mahuva movement filed Public Interest Litigations in the state High Court and then the Supreme Court of India to challenge the construction of the cement factory in the midst of productive, agricultural land. *Machimar Adhikar Sangharsh Samiti* (MASS) filed a Public Interest Litigation in the state High Court and lodged a complaint with the national Ministry of Environment and Forest to challenge the building of a power plant in a coastal area that provided livelihood and was designated an ecologically protected zone.

The success of the Mahuva movement, albeit a contingent one, versus the partial success of the MASS movement, however, shows that the same legal action does not necessarily lead to the same outcome. Other factors, such as the greater importance of a power plant versus a cement factory, the relationship of Modi to the two subaltern communities and their political allegiance (one Muslim and pro-Congress while the other Hindu and pro-BJP), and his relationship with the two corporations (constrained with Nirma due to lack of support in the previous election, while benign with the OPG), were among other factors that also played a part in the different results. Nonetheless, even MASS was able to pressure OPG to change its technology to one that will be less destructive of their livelihoods and the environment. The Sangathan's legalism from below did not involve the courts or the ministries, but used the Right to Information Act to educate and mobilize the *adivasis* against the construction of the dams.

Yet, scholars such as Nielsen (2011) have argued that for subaltern struggles against land acquisition, the letter of the law is not very meaningful and the courts have often been unresponsive, De facto endorsing displacements. And such legal action can be a form of co-optation, neoliberal governmentality, or a strategy to keep the subaltern groups appeased even as they are tied up in lengthy legal battles without substantially changing the model of accumulation by dispossession. The struggles in this book suggest that it is not so clear-cut.

In the case of both the Mahuva movement and MASS, the courts and the national ministry ruled in favor of the farmers and fishers, respectively, although recently, both groups faced fines for "excessive" use of the law. But even when unsuccessful, such strategies, by putting a stay on construction, buy time for subaltern groups and their advocates (e.g., Levien, 2013). And this, as Srivastava (2009) noted, favors the subaltern groups: "It is a battle of patience between the State and the people. And sometimes, people do hold out longer than the state expects them to" (cited in Levien, 2013: 365). As Levien (2013) notes, the centrality of a legal strategy in land struggles is inevitable and a historical fact. Moreover, as Comaroff and Comaroff (2009) suggest, legalism from below can undermine or subvert the legal fetishism of the neoliberal era.

Legalism from below, however, does involve a great degree of professional expertise, which some scholars argue can result in professionalization and de-radicalization of movements (e.g., Alvarez, 2009; Meyer and Tarrow, 1998; Piven and Cloward, 1978). Meyer and Tarrow (1998) argued that social movements were becoming more like interest groups and political parties rather than entities outside the political arrangement of power. Hence, they wondered whether the

> social movement as we have known it in the history of the West . . . [is] losing its power to surprise, to disrupt and to mobilize, and to provide a meaningful and effective alternative form of politics for those without access to more conventional means of influence.
>
> (Meyer and Tarrow 1998: 26)

The three struggles, along with others currently underway in India, suggest that this does not have to be the case. For legalism from below is more than legal court battles. It also engages subaltern groups, both men and women, in collective dialogues, truth commissions, and ground-truthing, as well as training workshops on human rights and social justice that facilitate their understanding of law as ontology. While these forms of legalism from below are often gendered and more likely to happen outside the struggle and within women's movement organizations (WMOs), they do suggest possibilities for law as social movements. Such legal citizenship, along with protest, sometimes enables subaltern groups to access state power that is usually not within their reach.

Such a multi-pronged repertoire, as I have shown in the previous chapters, was made possible by the growing experience and expertise of the translocal field of protest that had come into being over several decades. The successive waves of protest in India and Gujarat left behind an enduring social justice imaginary, a translocal protest infrastructure – of movement organizations; non-governmental organizations (NGOs); advocacy groups; networks; and legal, media, and academic supporters who can be mobilized when needed – along with a protest repertoire. In particular, many of the activists and supporters of the three struggles had been involved in the *Narmada Bachao Andolan* (NBA) and talked about its influence on their lives and work.

Such a translocal field of protest thus provides insights into the ways in which we think about social movement success and their long-term ripples on the political culture of the region. By some measures, the NBA was not successful, as the major dams were built and many of those affected are still not rehabilitated. But almost none of the supporters I encountered saw NBA in those terms. For them, NBA was a touchstone of what can be accomplished by subaltern protest. It changed the policy environment around such large-scale infrastructure development projects: resettlement and rehabilitation policies are now built into such projects, including in the new Land Acquisition Act, which was passed on March 10, 2015, by the *Lok Sabha* (people's house or the lower house of the Indian parliament). It also raised awareness among the larger public about the costs of development borne by subaltern groups.[2] More importantly, the call of "Vikas not Vinash" (Development not Destruction) that emerged from NBA now resonates in most subaltern struggles today, not merely as rhetoric but as a fundamental critique of the development model based on the dispossession of subaltern groups. Thus, as Schurman and Munro (2010) note, the measure of a movement's success and failure can more fully be understood in terms of "how movements matter" and their long-term influence on the political field.

This translocal field of protest, however, has some built-in tensions. On one hand, it enables subaltern struggles by subsidizing various organizational costs. Each struggle had formed a collective legal identity in whose name the struggle was fought, that is, Nar-Par Adivasi Sangathan, Mahuva Khetiwadi Paryavaran Bachao Samiti, and Macchimar Adhikar Sangharsh Samiti. But these were not entities with structures and staff that needed resources to be maintained. Movement anchors, other NGOs, and supporters in the translocal field of protest raised the necessary resources for a specific mobilization or action. Thus, the existence of a translocal field of protest has addressed an important dilemma of poor people's movements. But as I showed in the chapter on the Sangathan and MASS, the lack of a formal structure also meant that male elders and leaders often made decisions informally and excluded women, resulting in another form of "tyranny of structurelessness" identified by Jo Freeman (1972).

On the other hand, the translocal field of protest also facilitates a gendered division of labor and prevents intersectional thinking within struggles. In Gujarat, the main elements of this translocal field of protest were movement organizations and NGOs related to the Gandhian, feminist, farmers', and environmental movements. Although there are ongoing interactions among these movements, there is also a division of labor that precludes the development of an intersectional understanding and strategies within the struggles. This reduces gender issues to including women in the public spaces of the struggles, but not always in the decision-making spaces. It also precludes attention to how dispossession affects men and women differently and how that can be incorporated in the struggle. And even this limited way of incorporating women varied within each struggle based on the political commitments of the movement anchors and their relationship with WMOs in the local and translocal field of protest.

As shown in the preceding chapters, in the case of the Sangathan, the trust did not have an ongoing relationship with WMOs. Hence, when they engaged in the struggle, *adivasi* women had to challenge their exclusion from meetings and other spontaneous gatherings such as the people's court. In the Mahuva movement, the movement anchors were politicians and activists who saw subaltern women as strategically important to the public face of the struggle. Hence, they were included as speakers in public rallies and *yatras*, but like subaltern men, were seldom included in collective dialogues and meetings. MASS was anchored by a community-based organization that was explicitly committed to gender equality and had ongoing relationships with WMOs and included subaltern women and men not only in public hearings and rallies, but also in collective dialogues and meetings. But given the gender segregation of rural spaces, subaltern women were excluded from informal meetings and conversations.

Yet, in the Mahuva movement and MASS, WMOs like Utthan and Ujjas/ KMVS, respectively, challenge the struggles to think more inclusively, even if they don't always succeed. For example, MASS does engage subaltern women and men in ground-truthing and discussion of policy changes to work towards a gender-just perspective. Both the Mahuva movement and MASS also did nominate women to run for local elections under the reservation of 33% of seats. Unfortunately, in both cases, when subaltern women won the election for the position of *sarpanch*, it was a male relative who wielded most of the power. WMOs are providing ongoing political training to subaltern women and men to address such dynamics. More than training, however, it might necessitate what Spivak (2012) calls an aesthetic education the non-coercive training of the imagination for alternative epistemic performances that sustain justice and freedom. Also, all three struggles are building an expanded translocal field of protest against dispossession with other struggles in Gujarat and including subaltern women and men in some of these efforts.

But for subaltern and other struggles for social justice to be gender-just requires an ongoing commitment, expressed through practices and mechanisms that address gender justice. Based on a large-scale research project that analyzed the relationship between gender and social movements, Horn (2013: 5) suggests various ways for social movements to be gender-just. Among those are for social movements to recognize and explicitly name gender inequality and patriarchal power as a concern for all, and hence integral to all efforts for social justice; create space for reflection within the movement on women's rights and gender justice; provide active support for women's participation and leadership; consistently tackle gender-based violence within movement spaces; assess and address gender division of labor within movements; enable full participation of men and women in keeping with their care and reproductive responsibilities; and expect and address backlash faced by activists for engaging in gender justice work. The three struggles have undertaken some of these efforts. Albeit tentative, such efforts are hopeful signs for a gender-just development and democracy.

As such, they also contribute towards theorizing about subaltern struggles, development, and democracy.

Theorizing subaltern struggles, development, and democracy

The three struggles demonstrate a complex relationship between subaltern struggles, development, and democracy. To date, they have succeeded in preventing the construction of dams, ordering the dismantling of the cement factory, and pressuring the power plant to change its technology. But their efforts, along with those of many others, have not resulted in "enduring or large-scale social change as such" (McMichael, 2010).

Yet, all three struggles are engaged in such enduring efforts. For example, activists from all three struggles are currently participating in the state-level mobilization against the Special Investment Zone planned in Gujarat. Such mobilizations have not only raised awareness about the dispossession of subaltern communities, but also resulted in victories in other similar struggles in Gujarat. Moreover, as McMichael (2010) noted, such subaltern struggles are important locally where they address issues of survival and justice and translocally where they contribute to problematizing the dominant vision of development and progress. "By examining these struggles as expressions of development exclusions in this historical conjuncture, it is possible to specify development limitations and to identify the diversity of possible futures" (McMichael, 2010: 5). Among those development limitations are those of incorporating a fuller sense of gender justice beyond women's empowerment defined in narrow economic and political terms and that includes men.

Just as importantly, they also provide an alternative to the master frame of development in India. Writing about changing social movements in India, Ray and Katzenstein (2005) argued that the master frame of social movements changed from that of Nehruvian democratic socialism (1947–1964), to multiple frames that combined class with other identities of caste, gender, and environment (1964–1984), to the master frame of religious nationalism and market from the 1980s to the present. As a result, they argued, while there are

> still Medha Patkars protesting the displacement of impoverished villagers ... there is also, and with increasing visibility, important movement activism that is reconstituting their demands to accord with the changing times in ways that often do not foreground the concerns of the poor.
> (Ray and Katzenstein, 2005: 26)

Social movement politics, they concluded, remain an institutional site where anti-poverty language remains. But they wondered whether these movements would endure as the egalitarian conscience of India.

Nearly a decade since their question, as the three struggles in the book demonstrate, one can provisionally say that, at least currently, such egalitarian conscience has endured. But the frame that animates this conscience is Gandhian *gram-swaraj* along with the multiple frames of gender, caste, and environmental justice. Thus, the current state–society master frame of religious nationalism and market is not the only one. Furthermore, the importance of the translocal field of protest in each of the struggles suggests that

Towards gender-just development 137

not only did the egalitarian conscience endure, but so did the infrastructure of protest and translocal solidarities.

The struggles also challenge the theorization of subaltern politics as either a form of governmentality or radical democracy, and represent an attempt towards democratizing democracy even as they struggle with gendered geographies. For example, Partha Chatterjee (2004) theorized contemporary subaltern politics in India as reflecting governmentality within political society. He differentiated political society, as the domain for the management of non-corporate capital, from civil society in which corporate capital was hegemonic. This meant that subaltern populations, whether in the informal economy in the urban areas or peasants in the rural areas, were not seen as citizens with rights but part of political society to be governed for the benefit of those in civil society. The participants of all three struggles, however, saw themselves as citizens who had a right to challenge the injustice of their dispossession and exclusion from so-called development. Subramanian (2009) similarly argued that fishers in South India, by "transforming claims into rights through political maneuver, . . . actually forced a reconstitution of both governmental categories and legal frameworks and, by extension, the meaning of citizenship" (p. 23).

Chatterjee (2010) also differentiated between the politics and possibilities of urban versus rural subaltern groups. He argued that the politics of urban subaltern groups focused primarily around livelihood projects and were defined and succeed within the rules of the market and government regulation. The rural folks, however, were still dependent on the government for basic needs and unable to access the market in agricultural commodities. Thus, he claimed that peasant politics were more about demonstrating discrimination in accessing state-provided basic needs in the fields of education, health, and agriculture than of exploitation by the state. Again, the three struggles belie this, as all of them challenge the state's development project and demand their rights to land and livelihood rather than demand services. Moreover, the subaltern groups in all three struggles were also able to access the market through cooperatives, self-help groups, and producer companies.

While Chatterjee made a case for subaltern politics as governmentality, other scholars have theorized subaltern politics as a form of radical democracy that is anti-state and emerging from an autonomous cultural space not fully absorbed by capitalism and colonialism. Broadly, this perspective, articulated by Choudry and Kapoor (2010), Escobar (2008), and Whitehead (2010), among others, saw in contemporary subaltern movements an articulation of an alternative to development, drawing upon their indigenous differences and cosmologies. Here the state is decentered in favor of autonomous communities. Some have critiqued it as a form of soft orientalism or reproducing binaries of modern/traditional in a more sympathetic vein (e.g., Conway 2013).

The struggles in this book also challenge such a reading as they work both with and against the state and, to different extents, participate in projects of democratizing democracy, which range from *mahila panchayat*, to developing a rights-based plan for local development, to articulating with struggles across the country to engage in collective dialogues around social and political projects of transformation. And as Nilsen (2010) argues, while there are new subjectivities and multiple subaltern groups that organize across scales, the moral economy of rights, not difference, is still the basic architecture of the demands, even as difference – particularly of gender, caste, and religion – continues to haunt the struggles.

Finally, the gendered geography of the struggles also highlights the need to address the gender division of theorizing. It is still feminist scholars who pay attention to the ways in which the state, development, and democracy are gendered and the efforts of women's movements to address such gender inequalities. Non-feminist scholars may allude to gender, that is, women, but seldom incorporate a gendered analysis in their theorizing, thus implicitly if not explicitly reproducing a gender division of theoretical labor. But we can hope that highlighting such gendered geographies will lead towards a more gender-just development, democracy, and theorizing.

Notes

1 Though Professor Errol D'Souza, professor of economics at Indian Institute of Management-Ahmedabad, has noted that Gujarat is the second worst state in terms of enforcing contracts and the costs of enforcing them are also very high (DNA, 2015).
2 These changes were, of course, not only a result of the NBA, but also other factors including the global and national environmental justice regimes emerging from the 1972 and 1992 Rio and Rio plus 20 Summit declarations, to which India is a signatory.

References

Alvarez, Sonia. 2009. "Beyond NGO-ization? Reflections from Latin America." *Development* 52:175–184.

Chatterjee, Partha. 2010. "The State." *The Oxford Companion to Politics in India.* New Delhi: Oxford University Press.

———. 2004. *The Politics of the Governed: Reflections on Popular Politics in Most of the World.* New York: Columbia University Press.

Choudry, Aziz and Dip Kapoor, editors. 2010. *Learning from the Ground Up: global Perspectives on Social Movements and Knowledge Production.* London: Palgrave McMillan.

Comaroff, John, and Jean Comaroff. 2009. "Reflections on the Anthropology of Law, Governance, and Sovereignty." In *Rules of Law and Laws of Ruling*. Edited by Franz von Benda-Beckmann, Keebet von Benda-Beckmann, and Julia Eckert. Farnham: Ashgate.

Conway, Janet. 2013. *Edges of Global Justice: The World Social Forum and its Others*. London and New York: Routledge.

Escobar, Arturo. 2008. *Territories of Difference: Place, Movement, Life*, Redes. Durham: Duke University Press.

Freeman, Jo. 1972. "The Tyranny of Structurelessness." *The Berkeley Journal of Sociology* 17:151–165.

Horn, Jessica. 2013. *Gender and Social Movements: Overview Report.*. Brighton: BRIDGE/Institute of Development Studies.

Jeffrey, Robin. 2014. "Modi's Sweeping Victory in India," available at www.Inside.org.au.

Levien, Michael. 2013. "The Politics of Dispossession: Theorizing India's "Land Wars."" *Politics and Society* 41(3):351–394.

McMichael, Philip, editor. 2010. *Contesting Development: Critical Struggles for Social Change*. London: Routledge.

Meyer, David and Sidney Tarrow, editors. 1998. *The Social Movement Society*. Lanham: Rowman and Littlefield.

Nielsen, Kenneth. 2011. "Land, Law, Resistance," *Economic and Political Weekly* 46(41):38–40.

Nilsen Gunvald, Alf. 2010. *Dispossession and Resistance in India: The River and the Rage*. London: Routledge.

Piven, Francis Fox and Richard Cloward. 1978. *Poor People's Movements: Why They Succeed How They Fail*. New York: Vintage.

Ray, Raka and Mary Fainsod Katzenstein, editors. 2005. *Social Movements in India: Poverty, Power, and Politics*. Lanham: Rowman and Littlefield.

Schurman, Rachel and William A. Munro. 2010. *Fighting for the Future of Food: Activists versus Agribusiness in the Struggle over Biotechnology*. Minneapolis: University of Minnesota Press.

Spivak, Gayatri. 2012. *An Aesthetic Education in the Era of Globalization*. Cambridge: Harvard University Press.

Subramanian, Ajantha. 2009. *Shorelines: Space and Rights in South India*. Stanford: Stanford University Press.

Whitehead, Judith. 2010. *Development and Dispossession in the Narmada Valley*. London: Pearson.

Appendix: the Par-Tapi-Narmada Link Project

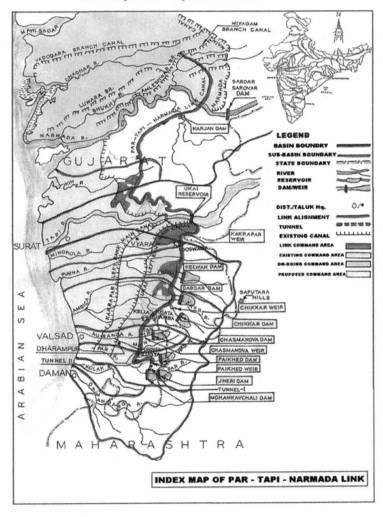

A.1 Par-Tapi-Narmada Link Project

Source: http://india-wris.nrsc.gov.in/wrpinfo/index.php?title=Par-Tapi-Narmada_Link

The interlinking of rivers is conceived as a means of regional water transfer to address the paradox of water surplus and deficit that exists in Gujarat and elsewhere in India (Pasi and Smardon, 2012). Such regional water transfers have a long history around the world and have been seen as an efficient way to address regional water inequality. In India, the inter-linking of rivers project was officially adopted by the Ministry of Water Resources of the government of India in 2002, following a Supreme Court ruling. The current project draws upon the dominant colonial policy of water resource management, that is, hydraulic manipulation of rivers (D'Souza, 2003) through engineering solutions such as dams and diversions.

Such a project had been proposed several times since independence. In 1972 Dr. K. L. Rao proposed the Ganga-Cauvery Link as part of a national water grid that would connect water-deficit and surplus regions. Another such scheme was proposed in 1977 by Captain Dastur to feed Himalayan water to peninsular India via pipelines (Pasi and Smardon, 2012). At the time, both these projects were considered impractical, technically and financially, but the idea made its way into the National Perspective Plan of the Ministry of Water Resources in 1980. The National Water Development Agency (NWDA) was created in 1982 to carry out feasibility studies for forty-two water transfer links proposed in the initial plan, twenty-one in the northern Himalayan region, and twenty-one in southern peninsular India (Pasi and Smardon, 2012).

A National Water Policy was formulated in 1987 to ensure a coordinated program. Another revised policy in 2002 divided the country into various water zones within which to move water from the surplus to deficit areas. In all these proposals, the main rationale for such redistribution was first to ensure water for drinking and irrigation and secondarily as a mechanism of flood control, power generation, and navigation. A task force was set up in 2002 to expedite the process, and according to the government of India timeline, feasibility studies, memoranda of understandings between states, and the construction would all be completed by 2016. But due to opposition from subaltern groups as well as from scholars and policy makers, although NWDA has been working on river link projects for the past two decades, they have disappeared from the 9th and 10th National Development Plans.

To date, while several feasibility studies have been conducted and some memoranda signed, very few links have actually been constructed. Preliminary feasibility studies for the Par-Tapi-Narmada Link were conducted in 2005, and a memorandum of understanding was signed by Gujarat and Maharashtra in 2008. Further topographic studies were begun in 2010 but have not been completed due to Sangathan protests. Hence, the project itself is currently on hold.

Since the 1970s, the rationality of water redistribution via large dams and river link projects has been challenged by subaltern groups who have been displaced from their land and livelihoods. The *Narmada Bachoa Andolan* (NBA; Save the Narmada Struggle) has been at the forefront of such challenges in India (e.g., Baviskar, 1995; Nilsen, 2010). Formed in 1985 to protest the building of several hundred dams on the Narmada River, the movement gained international fame when it forced the World Bank to withdraw its funding for the project based on its social and environmental costs. Unfortunately, the three states and the Indian government continued with the project, in the process displacing over a quarter million *adivasis* and submerging hundreds of villages with fertile land. Thousands of those displaced have still not been rehabilitated and so the movement continues on behalf of those *adivasis* and also in a new form, the National Alliance of People's Movement (NAPM), to fundamentally challenge the model of development based on dispossession of subaltern groups. Thus, from Nehru's temples of development, today subaltern groups see dams as harbingers of destruction and doom. In addition to loss of homes, land, and livelihood, they raise issues of distribution and equity that prioritize the needs of the urban population and industry over the rural majority that depends on agriculture. Finally, it is also important to consider the adverse environmental impacts – ranging from altering and fragmenting river flows and basins, disrupting ecosystems, loss of biodiversity through submergence and loss of forests, and loss of soil fertility.

Such protests have been informed and supported by academics and policy makers, who also question the very notions of surplus and deficit that are the basis of such projects. Critics call such formulations misguided and inaccurate, as they are based on a superficial understanding of the role of water in the ecology of a region. Pasi and Smardon (2012), for example, note that water surplus does not take into consideration the importance of that surplus for maintaining the local ecology, such as nutrient recycling and maintenance of wetlands. Similarly, deficit is assumed rather than demonstrated and is often a result of poor water management and unsustainable demands created by urbanization and industrial development. The superintendent of the NWDA office in Valsad, Mr. Gupta, confirmed this when he noted that rural folks need about 70 liters of water a day while urban folks need 200 liters. Hence, scholars argue that this analysis is driven by industrial development needs rather than promoting careful and sustainable practices within a water basin.

Yet, such thinking of scarcity/surplus informs most bureaucrats and engineers. For example, Mr. Gupta, who is in charge of writing the report and making recommendations for the Par-Tapi-Narmada Link Project, explained the rationale for the project as follows. He noted that the Dharampur area receives the highest rainfall in the state of Gujarat and most of this just flows via the rivers into the Arabian Sea, a process he saw as a "waste of rain water."[1] In addition to seeing the link project as a rational response to wasted surplus, he saw it as an ethical issue. He asked me: "Why would people in South Gujarat who are blessed with such surplus not want to share it with others who are not so lucky?" Moreover, he said, imagine the incalculable well-being and unanticipated rewards that *adivasis* will derive from the *duwa* (blessings of gratitude) of the folks from Saurashtra and Kutch. After all, "it is the law of nature to reward those who are generous."

While the project was justified primarily in terms of water redistribution, Mr. Gupta and engineers at the NWDA also argued that the *adivasi* communities also stood to gain from it. Right now, the rivers in the area run dry by March. So building the dams would first give them water for drinking and irrigation, and only the surplus would be given to the rest of the state. Furthermore, one of the administrators noted, migration is not necessarily always bad. Citing his own example, he said his family was from a district in North Gujarat, which was perpetually drought prone. Hence, many of his siblings and cousins left their ancestral village and sought education and jobs elsewhere and now enjoy successful lives in other parts of the state. Had they remained in their village, he observed, the same few acres of land would be divided into even smaller plots, making all their lives poorer. So why should the *adivasis* not have the same opportunities for migration and mobility? Comparing involuntary displacement and dispossession to voluntary migration obscures not only the elements of coercion and the lack of agency in the former, but also the realities of *adivasi* migration for decades. As Shah (2010) notes, for many *adivasis* migration is not only a means of augmenting livelihoods, but also freedom from social pressures in small communities. Hence, she is opposed to what she calls "eco-carceration," evident among many advocates and *adivasi* activists.

Among the other benefits to the local community noted by Mr. Gupta were the rehabilitation packages, which he claimed would more than adequately compensate them for any losses. When I mentioned that a decade later many displaced by the dams on the Narmada have still to be rehabilitated and ironically many don't even have adequate drinking water in the temporary camps where they have been housed, his response was that 90% of the people have been rehabilitated and are satisfied and there will always be some folks who will be disgruntled no matter what you do. Apart from questionable data, several independent studies show that more than 10% of people have not received compensation (e.g., Nilsen 2010); this logic not only advocates a majoritarian view, but dismisses subaltern loss as disgruntlement.

Thus, according to him this project was a win-win situation for everyone. So how did he explain the Sangathan's opposition? His response was the hand of "outside agitators." He said there are always people, activists, and non-governmental organizations (NGOs) who don't do their own work but obstruct others. They unnecessarily "agitate" the *adivasis* to question all government projects. He then recounted how at a meeting organized with the *adivasis*, "For every point we make they come up with ten other questions that we cannot respond to as our points are based on facts and data and theirs are not. We are technical people, we can only do so much convincing. It is like a patient who goes to a doctor but refuses to take any advice from him, so he will suffer." Technical rationality was thus his refuge to questions of social equity.

Furthermore, he suggested that such outside activists have vested interests and do not want the *adivasis* to benefit and develop as much as them. He then contrasted the vested interests of activists like Sujataben to his own commitment as someone not from the region but working for the benefit of the people in the area. But in the end, he noted with resignation, he had nothing to lose; he would soon be transferred and would leave behind a memo that he was prevented from completing his work by the protests in the community.

Note

1 Interview with Mr. Gupta, May 5, 2011.

References

Baviskar, Amita. 1995. *In the Belly of the River: Tribal Conflicts over Development in the Narmada Valley*. Delhi: Oxford University Press.

D'Souza, Rohan. 2003. "Supply-Side Hydrology in India: The Last Gasp." *Economic and Political Weekly* 38(36):3785–90.

Nilsen Gunvald, Alf. 2010. *Dispossession and Resistance in India: The River and the Rage*. London: Routledge.

Pasi, Nidhi and Richard Smardon. "Inter-Linking of Rivers in India: A Solution for Water Crisis in India or a Decision in Doubt?" *The Journal of Science Policy and Governance* 2(1):2–42.

Shah, Alpa. 2010. *In the Shadows of the State: Indigenous Politics, Environmentalism, and Insurgency in Jharkhand, India*. Durham and London: Duke University Press.

Index

Note: Page numbers with *f* indicate figures.

Action India 97
Action Research in Community Health and Development (ARCH) 68
Adani Corporation 104, 108, 118–19, 123, 125
Adivasi Ekta Manch 66
Adivasi Maha Sabha 69
adivasis 1, 18, 41; classifications of 52; exploitation/resistance history of 50–3; Forest Rights Acts and 51–2; Telangana movement of 27; women 15, 60–3
Anirudhbhai (activist) 89, 91
anti-statists 5
Appadurai, Arjun 11
Ayengar, Sushma 106, 121

Banarjee, Mukulika 8
bandar panchayats 109–10, 111*f*
Bayat, Asef 86
Bhadreshwar *Setu* (BSetu) 16, 105, 124–5; National Forum of Fishers and 112–13; Shekhadia movement and 109–10
bhajan (hymn) 90
Bharatiya Agro-Industries Foundation (BAIF) 64–6
Bharatiya Janata Party (BJP) 29, 130
Bhave, Vinoba 53, 67
bicycle *yatra*, Mahuva movement 94–6
Biggs, Michael 42
Blecher, Michael 10
Bouchard, Danielle 18

Center for Social Justice v. Union of India 33
Charkha (Spinning Wheel) 79
Chatterjee, Partha 5, 137
Chetrit, Joseph 90
Chhatra Yuva Sangharsh Vahini (Vehicle for Youth Struggle) 28
Chipko movement 28
choli 84
Choudry, Aziz 137
Coastal Regulation Zone (CRZ) Notification 113
coastal zone management plan (CZMP) 113
coercive nativism 26, 39
Comaroff, Jean 132
Comaroff, John 132
Committee to Save Farming and the Environment in Mahuva 78
Conway, Janet 13, 18
Corbridge, Stuart 3
Corporate Social Responsibility (CSR) initiatives 123

dalit 5, 28, 29
Debnath, Harekrishan 113
democracy, deepening of: decentralization and 30–1; legal architecture of 31; Panchayati Raj Act and 31–4; Right to Information Act and 36–8; social movement and 28–9
Desai, Jigna 18

Desai, Maniha 9
Detournay, Diane 18
Detox Corporation 114
Devi (goddess) movement 52
Dey, Nikhil 37–8
Dhamelia, Bavchandbhai 96
Dhammiben (activist) 84, 86
dharna (sit-in) 36
Dhattiwala, Raheel 42
D'Souza, Radha 27

Eckert, Julie 3, 8, 9
eco-carceration 144
ecology of knowledges 18
Environment Public Hearing (EPH) amendment 33
Eschle, Catherine 13
Escobar, Arturo 64, 137
Esteva, Gustavo 10
Excel Environ Solutions 48
Export Corporation 39

Featherstone, David 11
field of protest 11–12; elements of 11; legalism from below and 11–12; *Machimar Adhikar Sangharsh Samiti* formation and national 112–14; nested local, emergence of 105–7; Sarvodaya Parivar Trust local 67–9
fisher communities 108–12, 109*f*
Fojdar, Navnitbhai 53, 67
Forest Rights Act 52
Freeman, Jo 134

Gandhi, Indira 29, 34, 35
Gandhi, Mahatma 31, 38, 64, 67, 84–5, 86
Gandhi, Rajiv 29
Garibi Hatao (abolish poverty) 29
gendered geography of struggle 4, 50; challenging 63–7; Mahuva movement and 96–9; movement spaces and 14; *Nar Par Adivasi Sangathan* 60–3; scholarship on 12–13; state, social movements, democracy relationship and 6–8; of *yatras* in Mahuva movement 81
gender equality regime 7

gender-just struggle: development and democracy 130–8; geography of 120–3
gender mainstreaming 7
gender regime, concept of 12
ghagra 84
Ghassem-Fachandi, Parvis 125
Goetz, Anne Marie 37
Gohil, Shakti Singh 26
gram panchayat (village council) 10
gram swaraj (village self-rule) 4, 28, 78, 94, 100, 136
Great Adivasi Convention 69
Green Tribunal 1
ground-truthing 12, 118–20
Gujarat: *adivasi* exploitation/ resistance in, history of 50–3; Center for Social Justice in 33; challenging development in 131–5; corruption in 40; growth rates in 39–40; legal plurality in 10–11; map of 2*f*; MASS protest in Kutch 1; *Nav Nirman* student movement in 40–1; Nirma Corporation protest in Saurashtra 1; Sangathan protest in South 1 (*see also Nar Par Adivasi Sangathan*); struggles in, overview of 1–4; translocal field of protest in 38–44
Gujarat Lok Samiti (People's Committee) 15
Gupta, Akhil 6
Gupta, Dipankar 43

Hardiman, David 51, 52, 68
Harijans 41
Harriss, John 3
Heller, Patrick 30, 31
Horn, Jessica 13, 135

India: democracy in, social movements and 4–8; gender equality regime 7; legal pluralism in 9; nation building 4–5; state-society relations in 3; subaltern social movements in 1–4; women's movements in 14

Index 149

Indian state: nature of 26–31; Nehruvian model and 26–7; neoliberal model and 26–31; Supreme Court activism in 34–6
India Shining 4
interlegality 10
International Women's Day 88
International Women's Decade 7

Janata (People's) Party 29
Jani, Manishi 40
jan sunwais (public hearings) 4
Jayawardena, Kumari 6, 85
Jeffrey, Robin 130
Jenkins, Ron 37
Jessop, Bob 6

Kadviben (activist) 77, 83, 88, 91, 93, 96, 97
Kalsaria, Kanubhai 15, 76, 77, 84, 98; bicycle *yatra* and 94–5; songs sung by women to honor 89–91; sword presentations to 86–7
Kapoor, Dip 137
Katzenstein, Mary Fainsod 27–8, 136
Kaviraj, Sudipta 5
kedia 84
KHAM 41
Khedut Samaj (Farmers' Society) 79
Kheti Vikas Sewa Trust (Trust for Agricultural Development and Welfare) 119
kineaesthetic empathy 84
Kohli, Atul 27, 29
Kohli, Kanchi 113
Kshatriyas 41
Kumar, Shashikant 43
Kutch Mahilla Vikas Sangathan (KMVS) 14, 120–1

Laine, Sofi 84
legalism from below 1–20, 132–3; defined 3; democracy in India and 4–8; field of protest and 11–12; gendered geography of struggle and 12–16; legal categories and 3; legal pluralism and 8–11; *Machimar Adhikar Sangharsh Samiti* and 114–17; in Mahuva movement 76–81; methodology used for 17–19; opportunities for 3; subaltern social movements and 1–4
legal pluralism 9–10
Levi, Margaret 126
Levien, Michael 4, 43, 44, 70, 131, 132
Li, Lianjiang 8
License Monitoring Cell 39
Lobo, Lancy 43
Lodi, Ibrahim 103, 113, 114
Lok Adhikar Manch (People's Rights Forum) 115
lower-caste political parties 5

Machimar Adhikar Sangharsh Samiti (MASS) 1–2, 15, 96, 103–27, 134; changing dynamics within struggle and 123–6; gender-just geography of struggle and 120–3; ground-truthing and 118–20; legalism from below and 114–17; Lodi and 103; movement anchor for 16; national field of protest and formation of 112–14; as nested, local field of protest 105–7; overview of 103–5; as participatory/gender-inclusive activism 107–12; rights-based planning and 117–18; *Setus* and 105–7
Machimar Adhikhar Rashtriya Abhiyan (National Campaign for Fishers' Rights) 113
mahila panchayats (women's courts) 10, 97
Mahuva *Khetiwadi Paryavaran Bachao Samiti* 78, 134
Mahuva movement 1, 74–101; bicycle *yatra* of 94–6; gendered geographies of *yatras* in 81; gendered geography of struggle and 96–9; legalism from below in 76–81; movement anchor for 15–16; movement anchors,

gender justice and 99–100; overview of 75; *padyatra* from Mahuva to Gandhinagar 81–3, 82*f*; subaltern women in 83–94
Maiguashca, Bice 13
MASS *see Machimar Adhikar Sangharsh Samiti* (MASS)
Mazdoor Kisan Shakti Sangathan (MKSS) 36–8
Mazumdar, Veena 6
McFarlane, Colin 11, 12, 56
McMichael, Philip 136
McNeish, John Andrew 9
Mehta, Mona 26, 39, 42
Mehta, Pratap Bhanu 36
Mehta, Sanatbhai 15, 78, 93, 94–5, 99
Menon, Manju 113
Menon, Nivedita 6
Meszaros, George 8
Meyer, David 132
Ministry of Environment and Forest (MoEF) 1, 80
MKSS *see Mazdoor Kisan Shakti Sangathan* (MKSS)
Modi, Narendra 2, 4, 130–1
Motta, Sara 27
movement anchors 15; gender justice and, in Mahuva movement 99–100; for *Machimar Adhikar Sangharsh Samiti* 16; for Mahuva movement 15–16; for Sangathan protest in South 15
moving forward questioning 18
Mulqueen, Tara 9–10
Mundra Hit Rakshak Manch (Forum for Protection of Rights in Mundra) 118
Munro, William A. 133

Narayan, Jai Prakash 28, 41
Narmada Bachao Andolan (NBA) 3, 6, 41–2, 44, 53–4, 55, 133, 143
Narmada Valley Dams Project 41–3; *see also Nar Par Adivasi Sangathan*
Nar Par Adivasi Sangathan 1, 48–72, 134; challenging gendered geography 63–7; gendered geography of struggle 60–3; Gupta comments on 69–71; history of exploitation/ resistance 50–3; information to political education transformation 54–60; movement anchor for 15; people's court for water samplers 48–50, 49*f*; protest in South 1; resisting displacement and 53–4; *Sarvodaya* movement and 67–9
National Alliance of People's Movements (NAPM) 59, 143
National Campaign for People's Right to Information 37
National Forum of Catamaran and Country Boat Fishermen's Rights and Marine Wealth 112
National Forum of Fishers (NFF) 112–13
National Water Development Agency (NWDA) 48, 56–7, 142; *see also Nar Par Adivasi Sangathan*
Navnirman Abhiyan 105
Nav Nirman (reconstruction) movement 3, 26, 28, 39, 40–1
Naxalbari movement 28
Naya Marg (*New Direction* magazine) 79
Nehruvian model 26–8; Gandhi, Indira and 29; poverty and growth issues during 28; social movements during 27–8; Telangana movement of peasants and 27; total revolution and 28; unstable equilibrium and 27
nested, local field of protest, emergence of 105–7
new social movements 5; *see also* subaltern social movements
Nielsen, Kenneth 44, 132
Nilsen, Alf Gunvald 5, 6, 27, 138
Nirma Corporation 1
nongovernmental organizations (NGOs) 3–4, 11, 16; development, in Dharampur 68; in Mahuva movement 79

Non-Party Political Formations 28
Non-Resident Indian investment cells 39

O'Brien, Kevin 8
Occupy Wall Street movement 9–10
Olson, David 126
Om Prakash Group (OPG) power plant 1, 103–4, 104*f*; protest song 103; public hearing of 114–15
Omvedt, Gail 28–9
OPG power plant *see* Om Prakash Group (OPG) power plant
Osterweil, Michal 64

padyatra 1, 16, 74*f*; from Mahuva to Gandhinagar 81–3, 82*f*; photos of bruised/abused women in 87–8, 87*f*
Paine, Thomas 10
Panchayati Raj Act 3, 19, 122
panchayati raj legislation 31–4
Pariyavaran Mitra (Friends of the Environment) 77, 79
Par-Tapi-Narmada Link Project 53, 61, 131, 141*f*, 142–5
participatory/gender-inclusive activism, building 107–12
Paryavaran Surakhsha Samiti (Environment Protection Committee) 54
Pasi, Nidhi 143
Patel, Bharatbhai 107, 109–10
Patel, Girishbhai 78
Pathak, Ila 15, 78, 86–7, 88, 91–2, 99
personal laws 6
political field, defined 11
Popular Assembly of the Peoples of Oxaca (APPO), Mexico 10
power of presence 86
prabhat pheris (morning rallies) 41
Project Affected People (PAP) 33
protest, translocal field of, in Gujarat 38–44
Public Interest Litigation (PIL) 34–5

Rajamani, Lavanya 34, 35
Rakeshbhai (activist) 107, 109–10
Ramesh, Jayaram 117
Rao, K. L. 142
Rao, Narasimha 29, 32
Ray, Raka 11, 27–8, 136
rightful resistance 3
rights-based planning 117–18
Right to Information (RTI) Act 3, 19, 36–8, 54
Roberts, Alasdair 38
Robnett, Belinda 13
Roy, Aruna 37–8

salwar-kameez 84
Sangari, Kum Kum 6
Sangathan *see Nar Par Adivasi Sangathan*
Sangh, Jana 29
Sanghavi, Nagindas 29, 38
Santos, Boaventura de Sousa 9, 10, 18
Sarabhai, Mallikaben 91
Sarangi, Prakash 38
Sarvodaya (Welfare of All) movement 53, 67–9
Sarvodaya Parivar Trust 50; alcohol pledge and 67–8; in Dangs 69; in Dharampur 68, 69; local field of protest and 67–9; NWDA generated booklet by 56–60, 57*f*, 58–9*f*
Sarvodaya Parivar Trust 15
Scheduled Castes/Tribes 27, 32, 41, 52
Schurman, Rachel 133
self-help groups 97, 122
Sen, Ilina 7
Sengupta, Arghya 34, 35
Setus 105–7, 126
SEWA (the Self Employed Women's Association) 28
Shah, Alpa 52, 70, 144
Sharma, Aradhana 6
Shekhadia movement 109–10
Shelat, S. K. 78
sherwani 84
Sheth, D. L. 31

Shiyal, Bharatbhai 76
Shrimad Rajchandra *ashram* 68
Shukaitis, Stevphen 90
Sieder, Rachel 9
silent revolution 5
Singh, V. P. 37
Sinha, Assema 39–40, 43
Sinha, Mrinalini 88
Skaria, Ajay 52
Smardon, Richard 143
South Indian Federation of Fishworkers' Societies 112
Spivak, Gayatri 18, 135
state-centric scholars 6
subaltern politics 3; elements of 5
subaltern social movements: arguments about 4; democracy and, in India 4–8; field of protest and 11–12; gendered geography of struggle and 4, 7–8; in India 1–4; law use by 8–11; nonparty political formations 5; theorizing 135–8
Subramanian, Ajantha 6, 137
Supreme Court (SC) activism 34–6; critics of 35–6; middle-class bias of 35; Public Interest Litigation and 34–5
Sutton, Barbara 86, 89

Tarrow, Sidney 59, 132
Tataryn, Anastasia 9–10
Tilly, Charles 55, 91
total revolution 28
translocal assemblages 12
translocal field of protest 3, 26–44; defined 11; in Gujarat 38–44; Indian state and, nature of 26–31; movements associated with 12; Narmada Valley Dams Project and 41–3; overview of 26; *panchayati raj* legislation and 31–4; Right to Information Act and 36–8; solidarities and 11–12; Supreme Court activism and 34–6
Trust *see* Sarvodaya Parivar Trust

Ujjas Mahila Sangathan 120–2
United Nations First World Conference on Women 7
United Nation's International Women's Year 7
Usmanbhai (activist) 107, 109–10
Utthan 14

Vaid, Sudesh 6
Vaidya, Chunni 15, 78, 81, 88, 91, 93, 94
Voss, Kim 94

Whitehead, Judith 137
Williams, Michelle 94
Witsoe, Jeffrey 5
women: activism avenues for 97; *adivasi* 15; in civil rights movement 13; dress and description of 84–5; mixed-gender movements role of 12–13; movements, in India 14; photos of bruised/abused, in *padyatra* 87–8, 87*f*; representation and leadership roles of 13; self-help groups and 97, 122; songs sung by, to honor Kanubhai 89–91; subaltern, in Mahuva movement 83–94; at World Social Forum 13
women's movement organizations (WMOs) 4, 14–15, 75, 133
Women's World Conference in Beijing 7
Worker and Farmers Empowerment Organization *see Mazdoor Kisan Shakti Sangathan* (MKSS)
Working Group for Women and Land Rights 100

Yagnik, Achyut 40
Yagnik, Anandbhai 78, 116
yatras (marches) 4, 48, 49, 54, 61–3; bicycle, of Mahuva movement 94–6; in Mahuva movement, gendered geographies of 81; from Mahuva to Gandhinagar 81–3, 82*f*